Carolina Haints

Ghosts, Folklore, and Mysteries of the Old North State

DAN SELLERS &
JEFFREY COCHRAN

SCHIFFER
PUBLISHING

4880 Lower Valley Road • Atglen, PA 19310

Other Schiffer Books on Related Subjects:

Folktales and Ghost Stories of North Carolina's Piedmont,
Theresa Bane & Cynthia Moore Brown, ISBN 978-0-7643-3745-1

Ghosts of the North Carolina Shores, Micheal Rivers,
ISBN 978-0-7643-3471-9

Haunted Historic Greensboro, Theresa Bane,
ISBN 978-0-7643-3174-9

Designed by Molly Shields

Type set in Gecko Lunch/Cambria

ISBN: 978-0-7643-6245-3
Printed in India

Published by Schiffer Publishing, Ltd.
4880 Lower Valley Road
Atglen, PA 19310
Phone: (610) 593-1777; Fax: (610) 593-2002
E-mail: Info@schifferbooks.com

For our complete selection of fine books on this and related
subjects, please visit our website at www.schifferbooks.com.
You may also write for a free catalog.

Schiffer Publishing's titles are available at special discounts
for bulk purchases for sales promotions or premiums. Special
editions, including personalized covers, corporate imprints, and
excerpts, can be created in large quantities for special needs. For
more information, contact the publisher.

We are always looking for people to write books on new and
related subjects. If you have an idea for a book, please contact us
at proposals@schifferbooks.com.

Contents

AUTHOR NOTE

Each chapter comprises two sections. The first is that of the legend, based on a review of the literature; this is almost entirely the work of Jeffrey Cochran. Following a break in the narrative, the remainder consists of a more personal account, comprising field research, interviews, and the experiences of Dan Sellers.

ACKNOWLEDGMENTS

We'd like to start this book off the right way, by acknowledging the countless people who helped us along the way. Honestly, it would be impossible to truly account for everyone who has inspired us and motivated us to write this book. But it seems only fitting to thank the folks whose contribution is felt throughout these pages. Some of them contributed financially, some of them gave extensive interviews, and some of them simply showed us kindness and shared with us that which is perhaps most valuable—their time. In no particular order, we'd like to acknowledge the contributions of the following folks:

While visiting the Bostian Bridge in Statesville, we were fortunate to meet Mr. James B. Troutman, who showed us great kindness.

In Asheville, our research team befriended Brian Bloxsom and Christian MacLeod, who not only gave us one hell of a tour but spent additional time hanging out with us and showing us some of the neat artifacts in Joshua P. Warren's Mystery Museum.

We're very grateful to Billy Ray Palmer for spending so much of his day to speak with us and share his extensive knowledge on the Moon-Eyed People and Cherokee history, and to Terrisa Carringer for her patience in arranging our visit.

We'd like to thank Kelsey Baker, co-owner of Boojum Brewery along with Carl Mimms, who helped us add another level of complexity to a story we feared was lacking.

Mr. Henry Singletary of Bladenboro gave of his time and memory to recollect stories from nearly sixty years ago, to talk to us about his hometown.

We're also grateful to Suzanna Ritz of Korner's Folly for sharing her insights and time to tell us about what it's like to work in the "strangest house in America."

Marion Evans of Sandy Creek took the time to speak with us about their young town's very old connection to a famous folk legend.

Mr. Philip Howard, eighth-generation Ocracoke Islander, was kind enough to speak with us at great length and not only shared his personal insights but opened up new worlds of knowledge that we're still exploring.

We're grateful to authors Michael Renegar and Amy Greer for the signed copy of their latest book, which has been an invaluable resource in understanding the complexities of Jamestown's Hitchhiking Ghost. Michael died shortly before we submitted the final draft of this book to the publisher. He was a friend of the show, and we're saddened by his passing. I hope wherever he is, he's gotten the answers to those mysteries he's spent a lifetime seeking.

We're also grateful to Mr. Tom Beasley, who gave much of his time to once again recount his story about the hitchhiking ghost, which he's undoubtedly told hundreds of times. Thanks for making it fresh and lively!

We'd like to thank Josh Ingersoll of Mordecai Historical State Park and Mr. Nelson Nauss of the Ghost Guild for making arrangements and then changing plans to accommodate our needs. Special thanks to Franklin Vagnone and Blake Stevenson for sharing their time, their research, and their own stories of Old Salem and the creepy tales from friends.

We're grateful to Sue Walker and Kristen McDonald from Public Services at the Lewis Walpole Library at Yale University. They were able to provide a high-resolution photograph of the Nag's Head Portrait, which sits at the library as part of their collection.

We're still overwhelmed by the hospitality and kindness shown by Sherry and Tanner Dodge, who welcomed me onto their property and ended up with some new knowledge as a result.

We're thankful for the friendship of Larry Hobbs, who we've had the good fortune of meeting on several occasions, whose contribution was greatly appreciated.

We'd also like to thank Ms. Stephanie Griffin, not only for her contribution but for her friendship and continued collaboration.

Thanks again to Rebekah Jordan, a devoted listener of the podcast who shared with us when we needed it.

We'd especially like to thank Mr. Josh Garner, without whose contribution this book would not have been possible. To you, Josh Garner, we humbly dedicate this book.

I'd be remiss of my primary duties as a husband and a father if I didn't acknowledge the love, support, and patience of my beautiful and brilliant children and the sacrifices made by my devoted wife, Lauren. Without you, none of this would be possible, or worth it.

Last, I'd like to thank our supporters. Whether you're a one-time or a constant listener of *The Carolina Haints Podcast*, or if you've ever attended the Wreak Havoc Horror Film Festival or bought a ticket to see one of our films or bought a DVD, or even if you just liked and shared one of our posts on social media, we'd like to say, most sincerely, thank you.

INTRODUCTION

Welcome dear readers to the *Carolina Haints* book, a compilation and expansion of some of our favorite stories from North Carolina's rich and dark history. Let me begin by giving you a little bit of our own history. I technically started *Carolina Haints* in 2010, after embarking on my professional career the year before and finding that I had spent so much time developing my education and training that I had neglected doing things for leisure. My supervisor at the time suggested that I get a hobby, something to take my mind off work when I wasn't at work.

I've always been a big film buff, and the desire to make films was always there, but the opportunity and resources were lacking. After thinking long and hard about it, I decided to combine my desire for filmmaking with my love of local folklore. Although I should have been more concerned with the quality of the material I was producing, thanks to the advent of YouTube anyone was allowed to create pretty much anything and put it out there for the world to see. Armed with a crappy camera and a dozen or so books about North Carolina ghost stories, I set out to visit these places and record a travel blog—what they used to call a "vlog."

I had great fun doing these initial eight episodes, but to be honest, they weren't very good. In fact, every time I feel nostalgic and decide to go back and look at them, I can't help but cringe. The camera work was so shaky, the audio was amateur hour, and my voice was so young it's barely recognizable. I must've realized this opinion back then, because after the initial run I canceled the show and removed it from YouTube. It didn't help that the videos were getting me undue attention from folks who mistook my interest as an exercise in ghost hunting. I dabbled with the idea of ghost hunting in my early teen years but never really did anything about it. As an adult, I had grown to loathe the idea of paranormal investigation, so when *Carolina Haints* was mistaken for ghost hunting, I wanted to distance myself from it.

I abandoned the idea and decided to focus again on my career. After a few stressful years, I found myself once again with a burning desire to be creative and make something. This led not only to my first feature film, *Hank vs. The Undead*, but to the creation of my production company, Wreak Havoc Productions. On this first film, I didn't really know what I was doing, so I basically did as much as I could; I served as the director, the camera operator, the screenwriter, the producer, editor, and special-effects designer, and I even wrote some original music for the film. Since then I've met a group of very talented and dedicated individuals who excel in different areas that I've grown to rely on to help make films—folks such as Sammie Cassell, who would go on to become my producing partner. There's Zack Fox, a hell of a filmmaker, whose work as a cinematographer never disappoints me. I've often partnered with film composer Judson Hurd, whose work often brings a tear to my eye. And I've also come to rely on Jeffrey Cochran as a collaborator, coproducer, and a writer.

After a few years of making movies, running a film festival, and producing a comedy talk-show-style podcast with Sammie Cassell, I decided to get back to the roots of what had initially sparked my creative interests. Although I was no longer making a vlog about my travels across the state, my interest in the subject had never really subsided. I'm sort of like that artistically— if something has my attention, it's almost impossible to move away from it until I've seen it through. So I knew I wanted to get back into ghost and folklore storytelling but knew I wouldn't have the time to do the vlog idea the right way. With a growing family at home and multiple film projects shuffling at once, I realized the best fit for me and the company would be in the form of a storytelling podcast.

I explored several options, including writing the show myself, and I spoke with a few authors about working on this show until I was lucky enough to start reading Jeff Cochran's book, *Sympathy for the Devil*. I had been introduced to Jeff by Sammie, and we had conversed a bit by email before meeting in person to coproduce a short horror film called *Midnight Shift*. I knew Jeff was an interesting guy with a lot of potential as a filmmaker, but I didn't realize how creative and hardworking he was as a writer until I began reading his writing. I began picking Jeff's brain to see if he had any interest in regional folklore stories, and was pleasantly relieved to find that not only did he too share a love of these tales but was quite knowledgeable. His book collection on the subject rivaled my own.

I asked Jeff to begin working with me on writing a show, and I'm still grateful that he agreed. I pitched the idea to him that this would be something we could both work on at a leisurely pace, at our own time, at home. I told him this would be an easy and fun endeavor—at least the latter half was true. I don't want to speak for Jeff, but I'd imagine it's taken a great deal of his time and mental energy to thoroughly pore through our material to conduct the necessary research, not to mention the effort he puts into writing each script. Jeff's a very organized person, and that translates into the way he thinks and plans and writes. I don't know if working on the show has been fun for him, but I tell you now, it sure has been fun to read his writing.

My job on the podcast is twofold; I host and produce the show. Jeff and I collaborate on the content of each season, each of us choosing a few stories that we're passionate about, making sure there's good representation across geography and in the various categories. In the show's first season, our categories for episodes were either ghost stories, folklore tales, or unexplained mysteries. In the second season we added *dark history*, and in the third season we included *true crime*. Honestly, the categories aren't all that important—they're just a way for us to make sure we don't get too heavy in one area that we neglect another. Each season of the show should have a good balance.

So as the producer, I typically read his scripts as soon as they come in, and devour them with a big smile on my face. Sometimes, I'll do some additional research or include some personal note of my own. I may give a few rewrites here and there to make things a little easier to say out loud, but generally the show is almost completely in Jeff's words. The recording is always done by myself, alone at home, in the wee hours of the morning so I'm not disturbed by barking dogs or screaming kids. I've been accused of sounding tired in some early episodes, and this is why. But my routine has become one episode at a time in a quiet space—just me, my computer to record and edit, a microphone on a stand with a pop filter and sound guard, my script, and a hot cup of tea. Each recording typically takes about an hour to complete.

I then begin editing the recording, cutting out all of my many verbal gaffs and mispronunciations. I then look for the perfect musical accompaniment, typically a bit of a score from a favorite film or classical piece. In season 3 I began incorporating some sound effects to help give the show a richer soundscape for the listener. All in all, it usually takes about an hour per every five minutes of running time to successfully edit the show up to standards. Trust me, this was not the case in the beginning. Much like with the original iteration, I'm not necessarily super proud of the earliest episodes of the podcast. Like most TV shows that have been running for years, they tend to get better after they settle in for a few years. I always encourage new listeners to listen to the latest episodes of the show and to work their way backward. The show's numbers tend to suggest that new listeners usually start at the beginning. All I can say to that is this: if you didn't care for the quality of the first few episodes, I didn't either. Don't get scared off; the show gets better as it goes. That's not to say that I'm so much better of a producer/narrator than I was a few years ago, but it means I put more time and effort into it than I once did. With the high quality of Jeff's writing, it deserves nothing less than my very best effort.

After each episode is written, recorded, and edited, my job then becomes creating artwork and descriptions to go with each episode, uploading it to our server, and scheduling its release. Once an episode is out there, my job still isn't done. I promote each episode through social media by sharing it and sometimes making promo materials, much like I would for a film. By the time I've worked diligently on producing an episode of *The Carolina Haints Podcast* and have seen it through to this point, it's time to start again. Sound exhausting? It is.

In case you thought I've forgotten the missing ingredient to this recipe, trust me, I haven't. That would be the amazing theme music composed, performed, mixed, and edited by Judson Hurd. The original theme he created for the first two seasons, titled "Dream," not only is a great fit for the show but is a beautiful, mysterious, and haunting piece of stand-alone music. I'm even happier with the second theme he's developed for the show, which began with the podcast's third season. It's a bit more playful and enigmatic than its predecessor and encompasses the feel of the later season's inclusion of true crime. This show wouldn't be what it is without Judson, and I'm truly in his debt.

So, skip ahead to three years of working on *The Carolina Haints Podcast*, all while still managing our annual international film festival (of which Jeff is a prolific judge), and still producing multiple film projects per year. Our listenership has grown exponentially since we started. Don't get me wrong; we're not breaking onto the iTunes list of top podcasts, but we've managed to get more downloads than most new podcasts do, and the average for each episode well establishes us in the top half of listenership for podcasts. So me being me, I never like to leave a good thing alone. I'm always pushing to improve and expand where possible. When I came to Jeff with the idea of adapting the show into this book, his rational and organized mind looked at it a bit skeptically. But being the good creative partner he was, he heard me out and kept an open mind.

I think I sold him on the idea of the book not just being a rehash of what listeners could get with the show, but an expansion of those stories with a personal account of each place. In other words, it wouldn't be enough to just publish our scripts in the form of a book. I wanted to go back to the roots of *Carolina Haints* and give readers an inside look—not only of what each location is like to visit, but what it feels like. I realize how intangible this may sound, but just bear with me. There's an essence to these stories that's hard to put into words. I can still remember the feeling I had as a kid when I picked up one of these North Carolina ghost books. I can't remember where I was or all the stories I read, but I can vividly remember the special feeling I felt deep inside while reading them. It's a feeling of excitement and potential and, oddly enough . . . of belonging.

While I enjoyed books like *Scary Stories to Tell in the Dark*, they didn't come close to capturing my imagination like local ghost-story books did. I think it has something to do with the idea that these stories are somehow linked to history and to a place—a real, tangible place, where people live and work and visit. Something about that notion thrilled me to my core as a child. That's what I wanted to convey with this book. I wanted to recount for the reader what it was like to go to these places and see them for myself. You see, I'm the kind of guy who will walk into a haunted house all alone on a cold, rainy night, on the anniversary of the tragedy that befell the poor soul twenty years ago, just to feel that rush of emotion. That depth of feeling is what inspires me to tell ghost stories and folklore legends, and it's what inspired me to cowrite this book.

In early 2020, Jeffrey Cochran and I set out on a research trip with our producing partners (and just good friends) Chad Hunt and Sammie Cassell. We traveled hundreds of miles across this state to some of the haunted locations that we've written about in this book. This was one of the best experiences of my life. Not only was I able to visit a few places I've never had an excuse to visit before, but I was able to gather some great research for this book, and, most importantly, I was able to spend time with friends who made me laugh so hard my head hurt. We encountered everything from heavy snowfall to practically getting lost in the mountains without a cell signal, but none of it seemed to matter because we were all doing what we wanted to be doing. We got to visit these incredible places as a group, each one of us as big of a smart ass as the next, cracking jokes at every opportunity, creating inside jokes that would last for years. It was a trip that I wouldn't trade for anything. And we intended to do more—except then the coronavirus hit the US, and that quickly put an end to our plans. I was able to carry on with a lot of the research, but it robbed us of the experiences that might've been. Perhaps future trips will have to be included in additional volumes of *Carolina Haints* in years to come.

Regardless of the experiences of our group, which I'll fondly refer to as "the Research Team," I had already been to many of the places covered in the book. Some of these travels were for the sole purpose of visiting haunted locations. Sometimes they were quick detours while taking my wife on a date. A few of them I've lived close to and have frequented often over the years. After all, like my grandmother used to say, I'm a Tar Heel born, I'm a Tar Heel bred, and when I die, I'll be a Tar Heel dead. I have an abiding love of the state of North Carolina—my home.

There's so much to see and do here, and such a diverse array of landscape and experience and history too. This is a wonderful place. Early English colonists came here to settle the New World. Orville and Wilbur Wright came here to invent manned flight. In one day you can experience a sunrise overlooking the Atlantic Ocean, then enjoy a busy city skyline; you can go from wide-open fields and farmland to expansive lakes and forests; and eventually you can make it to the heart of Appalachia in time for a golden sunset. Along the way you could meet some of the kindest, warmest, most interesting people you could imagine. You could eat some of the finest food in the world, hear some of the greatest music, hike some of the best trails, and still experience just a fraction of what North Carolina has to offer. Okay, I'm done sounding like a travel brochure for state tourism, but everything I've written is true, and I mean *every* word of it.

If you're from the Old North State or are able to spend any length of time in it, you may find that there's also a dark side to this place. There's a pretty deeply seated air of mystery that envelops this state. There's a rich history here going back five centuries and beyond, and not all of that history is pretty. In fact, some of it is downright brutal. Certain towns have given rise to tales that have endured through the decades. These tales are passed down orally from one generation to another. Some stories barely register, and finding any sort of sign that they ever existed is close to impossible, but some are so significant to a place and a people that it's part of their very fabric. These stories have stood the test of time and have stuck with us like a bad rash. The very stories themselves have haunted us and never let us forget that no matter what we tear down and build in its place, the story itself is still there looming in the shadows. That's what *Carolina Haints* is about—the things that haunt us.

One question I often get asked is, What's a "haint"? This is a term I grew up hearing and have just always known, and it sometimes baffles me that even native North Carolinians or other southerners might be unfamiliar. A *haint* is a southern colloquialism for a ghost or spirit. In the context of the show and now this book, a *haint* refers to the things that haunt us. I don't care who you are, we're all haunted by the ghosts of our past, whether it's regret or guilt or just plain fear. To put this sense of the word in the context of history and folklore is perhaps the best description of *haint* that I can offer, at least in the framing of this book.

The next-most-frequently-asked question I receive is if I believe in ghosts. I think so. If you had asked me twenty years ago, the answer would have been a resounding Yes! Five years ago, it would have been more like "I don't know." I think perhaps the best response I can give comes from the office wall of my favorite TV detective of my adolescence, and that's "I want to believe." I so want to believe that not everything has been explained; that there's still some mystery left in this world. I want to believe that we continue to exist after our body dies. I've always been intrigued by the way my high school English teacher put it: "I don't have to believe in ghosts to be afraid of them."

In other words, there's power in the stories.

I invite you now, dear reader, to embark with us on a journey from one end of this great state to the other. I want you to get into a dark, quiet place, maybe put on some creepy, droning background music, light a candle or two, and join us as we tell the macabre tales of *Carolina Haints* . . .

—Dan Sellers

There's plenty more that I could add here. How Dan inadvertently inspired me to begin writing. What the friendship of Dan, Sammie Cassell, and Chad Hunt has meant to me. And, of course, my own personal beliefs in the paranormal; along with a few personal stories.

BUT.

After Dan's long-winded diatribe, I doubt many of you have stuck around to be reading this . . . so I'll just save all that stuff for the next book.

—Jeffrey Cochran

PART I

Mountain Legends

CHAPTER 1

The Brown Mountain Lights

Linville, North Carolina

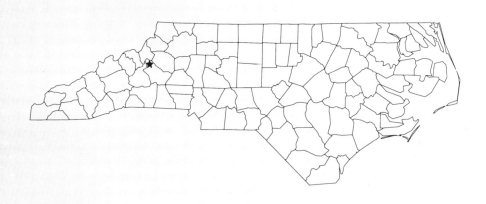

PODCAST • SEASON 1 • EPISODE 1
(September 22, 2017)

Western North Carolina is home to the highest US peak east of the Rockies, Mount Mitchell. There are many other well-known peaks in the area as well, but arguably the most famous of all is Brown Mountain. It isn't a particularly high peak; nor does it have any spectacular rock formations to boast about. Heck, it's barely a "mountain" at all, standing a mere 2,600 feet in elevation. There are several, perhaps more interesting, attractions around the area: the Mile High Swinging Bridge at Grandfather's Mountain, Linville Gorge and Linville Falls, and Table Rock or Linville Caverns.

Instead, Brown Mountain is best known for the mysterious lights that appear on and above its slopes. The Brown Mountain Lights are perhaps the most prevalent, best-documented, unexplained phenomenon in North Carolina. People come from all over the world to witness the flickering, dancing lights. Scientists have failed to find a plausible natural cause, and locals have invented legend to explain the event. No one seems to know exactly what they are or where they came from, but one thing is for certain: the Brown Mountain Lights are real and appear with remarkable regularity.

The lights manifest in a variety of ways. Sometimes they flash into existence and then disappear just as quickly as they came. At other times they linger, gliding along a ridge or rising into the sky before winking out. Sometimes they move in repetitive patterns, and other times they blink in and out, seemingly at random. Sometimes there is a single light, sometimes there are several, and occasionally there are more than you can count. Sometimes they rise, growing larger as they do, then burst in midair like silent fireworks. Even the color of the lights is a point of contention among witnesses. Some report a red light, others blue, but white or yellow lights have also been reported. Regardless of the color or the amount of lights, everyone agrees that the origin of the light is a mystery.

There are as many theories about the lights as there are manifestations. Residents say the lights started in 1850, when a local woman disappeared. Everyone believed that her husband had killed her and hid the body somewhere on the mountain. Blood was found at the scene, but the man claimed it was from a pig he had slaughtered. Without a body, no one could prove otherwise, so the locals began an extensive search for the body. They claim that the lights began to appear to help them in their search. In some versions of the story, the lights lead them to the woman's body, and in other versions, the body was not found, which is why the lights still persist today.

There is also the story of a pioneer family. The father left to serve in the Revolutionary War and, upon returning home, found the house burned to the ground. There was no sign of his family. The man searched the woods of the mountain day and night, using a lantern at night. After days without rest or food, he collapsed and died on the mountain. Many believe that the lights are his spirit still searching for his family.

Of course, other theories also exist. Some are variations on the searching legend, such as the spirit of a devoted slave whose master disappeared while hunting on the mountain. Day and night, the slave searched for his master until he himself lost consciousness and died. Even in death, he continues to search. Another variation is the one about the spirits of Catawba and Cherokee women searching for their husbands who had been lost in battle. That's the one I always heard growing up.

Other theories claim divine power and even UFOs.

Scientists have come up with their own theories—none of which hold any more merit than the local legends. In fact, the various scientific papers often contradict and disprove one another. Dozens of local scientists and would-be detectives have searched in vain for an answer to the mystery. On a few occasions, the Brown Mountain Lights have even attracted the attention of the United States government.

The first theory came in 1913, when the United States Geological Survey (USGS) concluded that the lights were nothing more than locomotive headlights seen over the mountain from the surrounding peaks. Even in an age when the public trusted the government implicitly, this answer did not satisfy very many people. Then, in 1916, the area was hit with massive flooding that knocked out all electrical power in the area for quite some time. It also destroyed several bridges, disrupting train service for weeks. Yet, during this time, the Brown Mountain Light events continued. After that, even the few who had believed the USGS explanation were forced to admit that there was no way that the lights could be from a passing locomotive.

In 1919, the mystery was presented to the Smithsonian Institution, which deferred the matter to the United States Weather Bureau. After a rather short and cursory investigation, they dismissed the lights as a weather phenomenon known as Andes Lights, which are formed when the extremely tall Andes Mountains cause silent electrical discharges to form in passing clouds; however, the Andes mountain range is *nine* times the height of the 2,600-foot Brown Mountain. Also, the lights are not seen on nearby Mount Mitchell, which dwarfs Brown Mountain at just under 6,700 feet.

In 1922, the USGS ordered a second, more extensive investigation. The ensuing report addressed, and dismissed, most of the theories that had been presented by other investigators up until that time.

On page 1 of the new report, the author reiterates the findings and the flaws of the 1913 study. A few pages later the report discusses, and for the most part disregards, other theories that investigators (whether local ones or government investigators) have presented. These can be divided into four categories: natural phenomena, chemical reactions, meteorological events, and man-made causes.

Natural phenomena include will-o'-the-wisps (marsh gas) and fox fire (phosphorescence). But, as the author points out, there are no swamps or marshes on Brown Mountain, and fox fire is much too faint to be seen at any distance.

Others have suggested chemical reactions such as free-state phosphorus, radium, or a combination of hydrogen, sulfide, and lead oxide, but this would break the laws of physics. Phosphorus does not exist in free state, and radium does not emit visible light. The third suggestion is just grasping at straws, since those elements have not been found on the mountain.

The lights have also been attributed to meteorological events, such as St. Elmo's fire and desert mirages. St. Elmo's fire happens only during thunderstorms, while the Brown Mountain Lights are best viewed on clear, stormless nights; therefore, the mirage theory has been generally accepted as the most feasible explanation. This theory says that air currents of different and unequal densities can produce a reflective surface that mirrors the light from the brightest stars. As strange as it may sound, this theory has never been completely disproven as far as I am aware.

And that leaves man-made causes. The author of the 1922 report revisits locomotives and automobiles, this time glossing over obvious flaws in the theory. Then, inexplicably, he presents his conclusions. He says that about half the lights are automobile headlights, a third are locomotive headlights, and the rest are stationary (electric) lights or brush fires.

What?

In the eyes of the United States government, the matter is "case closed." There have been no further official investigations in nearly one hundred years!

To that I say: What about Brahm? No, not the classical composer from the 1800s. Before him there was Gerard Will de Brahm, a German engineer. Brahm came to North Carolina in 1771 to conduct a survey of the Brown Mountain area. He was the first to make an official record of having seen "strange lights on a distant ridge." And, in 1771, neither the locomotive nor the automobile nor electric lighting had been invented. Yet, the US government maintains that these sources account for 90 percent of the Brown Mountain Lights sightings.

The Native Americans in the area say that the lights have existed for centuries. Cherokee legend tells of a great battle that took place between the Cherokee and Catawba tribes. The two Indian nations fought fiercely on the slopes and ridges of Brown Mountain some 800 years ago. Scores of brave warriors from both tribes were killed. When their husbands and loved ones did not return after the battle, the women took up torches and searched the hills for their bodies. The Cherokee say that shortly after this, the lights first began to appear.

Much like everything else about the Brown Mountain Lights, there are even conflicting views on the best place to witness the lights. Some recommend the Brown Mountain Overlook on NC 181, others prefer Lost Cove Cliffs Overlook, but most agree that Wiseman's View Overlook is the best spot.

Wiseman's View? As in Scott Wiseman? I haven't been able to confirm that information, but it seems likely. So, who is Scott Wiseman? He was an American singer/songwriter who was born in Spruce Pine, North Carolina, in 1909. Spruce Pine is about 20 miles northwest of Brown Mountain. In 1963, Wiseman recorded a song called "Brown Mountain Lights." Since then, at least ten other artists have rerecorded the song, including Acoustic Syndicate and Roy Orbison.

The Brown Mountain Lights have also been featured in popular TV shows such as *Ancient Aliens*, *Weird or What?*, *Mystery Hunters*, and *The X-Files*. They also made an appearance in Kathy Reichs's book *Speaking in Bones*, and in the 2014 feature film *Alien Abduction*.

DAN'S STORY

I grew up hearing tales of the Brown Mountain Lights, and since I was a young boy I've been fascinated. I remember hearing about the ghostly lights from my grandmother, who was a very religious and spiritual woman. She had a brilliant way of telling stories that would spark my imagination and undoubtedly left a long-lasting love of the mysterious and unexplained. Even my father, a graduate of Appalachian State University, told me he took a trip with some college friends one evening and saw it.

I didn't make the trek to the Linville Gorge to see the lights until I was an adult. I went with my wife (then girlfriend) in the fall of 2008. We stayed at a cabin in West Jefferson for the weekend but made the hour-plus drive to Linville. From having done some cursory research, we decided to go to Wiseman's View to spend the evening. We planned ahead—a full thermos of steaming black coffee, a basket of sandwiches and Danish, hoodies, coats, blankets, and, most importantly—a telescope. Not a fancy one—a cheap-o telescope only good for looking at the moon—something a broke grad student could afford.

Cell phone reception is not so great in this area, and relying on GPS to find your way can be a recipe for disaster, so we found directions to Wiseman's View and printed them out. We followed our directions to the letter and still had to stop and turn around a few times. Despite the ghostly appearance of the lights, traveling to and from our destination was by far the most frightening aspect of the story.

You kind of expect winding mountain back roads to be difficult to drive, but in our college two-wheel drive, this was a nearly impossible feat. The roads, or should I say *dirt paths*, seemed hopelessly steep. A few times we thought we were goners, as the threat of sliding back down the side of the cliff loomed. For someone who already had issues with heights, this was no picnic. We kept pushing forward, though, and eventually made it to the top of a hill, and as improbable as it seemed, there was a nice parking lot just for visitors of Wiseman's View.

We parked and gave each other a celebratory hug to have made it. After using the public facilities (it was either that or the bushes), we began making our way down a well-defined footpath. We didn't take any of our gear because we just wanted to see what we were dealing with first. We made the trek down the paved path, which turned into a dirt path and eventually into a stone platform. We finally made it to the observation deck and were breathless, but not from the hike. This stunning view was one of the most beautiful natural sights I've ever encountered and is etched into my memory to this day.

Imagine a beautiful mountain vista with enormous peaks and valleys, stretching from one side of the periphery to the other, emblazoned with the most perfect coloring of gold, red, brown, yellow, and green foliage. It was an incredible sight to behold. I took several photos from an old point-and-shoot pocket-sized digital camera, and we made our way to the multiple viewing areas. There were a handful of other people there who also were in awe of the magnificent sight. Had we not seen the ghostly lights that night, the trip would have been well worth it just for the view at dusk.

We got there just in time, because in less than an hour we were engulfed in darkness. If you're not familiar with western North Carolina at nighttime, then allow me to emphasize—when I say darkness, I mean complete and total darkness—especially in this sparsely inhabited area, with no illuminated homes, very few headlights, and no annoying light pollution from a nearby city. Without a flashlight, we wouldn't have been able to find our way back to our vehicle.

Once we were in place with our blankets and telescopes and gear, we settled in and waited. Despite all the stories, the internet articles, and even YouTube videos, we still didn't know what to expect. They say that the lights appear with much regularity, but given my luck, this would be the time they decided to take the night off. We waited with eager anticipation and stared into the dark void.

We didn't have to wait long. Almost at once, various spots across the mountainside and the creek bed were illuminated by the mysterious lights. They could easily be seen with the naked eye, but to say they lit up the mountain would be an exaggeration. The lights appeared to slowly move, but at such a distance it's very possible they were moving faster than my mind could comprehend. What I saw were lights of various colors—blue, white, yellow, green. Some stood still and faded away; some grew brighter and moved around.

When I was able to catch them with the use of my telescope, it appeared that they were a swarm of small balls of light. The best thing I can compare them to, through the magnified lens, would be a large horde of lightning bugs—but not the normal, everyday fireflies like you're likely to see in the warmer months. These were large, brightly glowing things that seemed to move in a whirlwind. From a distance they just looked like a blob of light—one solid yet translucent entity. But with the enhancement, a different story emerged.

I heard skeptics say things like "That's just a campfire from hikers in the gorge." While they're entitled to their opinion, this grown-up Boy Scout with dozens of camping trips under his belt has never seen a blue or green campfire. I think some folks are just so uncomfortable with something mysterious that they're forced to assign some logic or reason, at least in their own mind.

I don't know if the lights are supernatural or a natural phenomenon that we've yet to understand. If I could tell you, I'd certainly be ruining it for future generations. Considering the lights have been seen and documented for centuries, there's no reason to think they won't continue on for years to come. After this inaugural trip, my wife and I returned once again in 2012. This time we had only a pair of binoculars, and, unfortunately, there were not as many lights visible that time. But I'll never forget that experience, and no subsequent visit could ever dampen my memory and the exhilaration of finally seeing something truly unexplainable.

Perhaps there's something to be said for Friedrich Nietzsche's famous quote: "He who fights with monsters might take care lest he thereby become a monster. And if you gaze for long into an abyss, the abyss gazes also into you." This encounter changed me and helped forge the person I am today—a man thrilled by facing the unexplained, not only comfortable but delighted with the idea of mystery. I'm fine with the notion that the Brown Mountain Lights are unexplained phenomena—surely, if there ever was a credible explanation offered, it wouldn't be as fantastic or beautiful as what's left to the imagination.

Would I go back?

In a heartbeat—but with a four-wheel drive.

CHAPTER 2

The Boojum
Waynesville, North Carolina

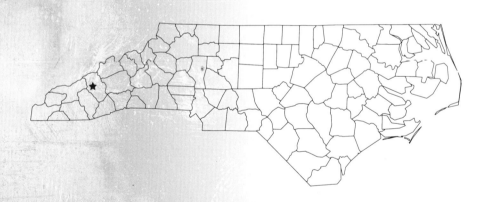

PODCAST • SEASON 2 • EPISODE 2
(October 5, 2018)

On the southern end of the Balsam Mountain Range is Eagle Nest Mountain, near Waynesville, North Carolina. At the turn of the last century (1900), a wealthy Waynesville businessman built a luxury hotel on the mountain called Eagle Nest Hotel. Guests at the hotel began to hear strange noises from an unusual creature that roamed the surrounding area. Some even claimed to see the strange beast firsthand. Mostly, though, were the feelings that people experienced. Hikers would report having the distinct feeling they were being watched, or, having heard a rustling in the trees, turned to find nothing but a swaying branch or a half-seen shadow.

The Balsam Mountain Range is home of the Boojum. The Boojum has been described as half man, half ape, half bear, half raccoon, and yet also as none of these. It's simply . . . the Boojum. It stands 7 to 8 feet tall and is bipedal. It's covered in shaggy brown (or gray) fur, except for the face, which is reportedly very humanlike. Its eyes are almost always described as sad and soulful.

It generally vocalizes itself through grunts and lip-smacking, but the screams can be heard echoing from ridge to ridge through the warm summer nights, or resounding ominously in the misty, fog-filled darkness of autumn. The screams are described as something of a mix between a hooting owl and a monkey or the growl of a tiger.

Sounds like a Bigfoot, right? Sounds like it, but it isn't—at least not really.

North Carolina does, indeed, have Bigfoot reports, but the Boojum has a couple of qualities about it that no Sasquatch has ever demonstrated.

First is its love of gems and, in fact, anything shiny. It's said to hoard glass bottles or moonshine jugs, but it mostly loves searching the clear mountain streams for gemstones such as rubies, emeralds, amethysts, and sapphires. It would store the gems inside the glass bottles and bury them in one of the numerous caves hidden throughout the Appalachian Mountains.

Now, this was backwoods country, especially in the early 1900s, so only the richest people had running water. Most "mountain folk" would bathe in a secluded spot in the stream or under a waterfall. The only thing Boojum loved as much as hunting for North Carolina rubies was spying on the local girls while they bathed themselves. It was not unusual for a girl to strip down, lower herself into a cool, mountain spring, and hear something rustling in the bushes. Most of the time it was a bird or a squirrel, sometimes it was a rabbit or mouse, but once in a while the girl would look up to find the hairy face of the Boojum staring back at her. The girl would inevitably scream, jump out of the water stark naked (much to the delight of the shameless Boojum), gather up her clothes, and run away.

Then there was Annie. When Annie found the Boojum peeping at her, she did not run. She looked into the big, brown eyes of the beast and simply saw another mountain creature. In fact, Annie began to feel so much for the Boojum that *she* sought *him* out and proceeded to court him! Before long, she left her family and her home to go live with the Boojum deep in the Appalachian woods as his wife.

The legend says that Annie and the Boojum loved each other deeply; however, the Boojum never lost his desire for rubies and emeralds. He would leave for days on end, searching for gems in the Balsam Mountain streams. The Boojum couldn't talk but made shrill noises and screams—as I said earlier, they were described as part hooting owl, part monkey—and when Annie would get lonely during the Boojum's long trips from home, she would go out to a clearing and howl for him to return. She became known to the locals as that crazy "Hootin' Annie," but she didn't care, because, more often than not, a similar scream would be heard from deep in the woods. Back and forth, Annie would scream to her Boojum, as he followed the sound back home to his beloved.

Now, as fun and far-fetched as this tale sounds, it has at least some basis in reality. The calls between Annie and the Boojum were frequently heard by guests of the Eagle Nest Hotel. The luxury hotel boasted many prominent and well-to-do patrons. Fearing that the Boojum may drive away business, the owner, S. C. Satterthwait, organized several Boojum hunts. Very little documentation exists about what happened next, but on April 22, 1918, the hotel burned to the ground.

Did Satterthwait succeed in killing the Boojum? Did a lonely and heartbroken Annie exact her revenge by burning down the building? Did Annie bear the Boojum children? Since the Eagle Nest Hotel fire, the Boojum has not been sighted nearly as frequently, but reports are still made to this day of strange noises and creatures in the woods and an unshakable feeling of being watched.

Folklore experts agree that Annie's owl-like screech was the source of the term "Hootenanny." It appeared around the turn of the twentieth century and originally meant any kind of party or get-together but was almost exclusively used to describe a get-together of rural or country folk. In the 1960s it came to mean specifically a gathering of musicians and was introduced to a larger swath of the population thanks to the music of Pete Seeger and Woody Guthrie.

DAN'S STORY

We visited Waynesville as part of our research trip. We knew going into it that the town didn't particularly have much to offer in the way of Boojum-inspired things to see and do, except for one place in particular. Boojum Brewery is located in the heart of town, in the middle of a busy street. If you're ever in the area and looking for a good burger, you could do a lot worse. Of course, I ordered the Boojum burger and the Boojum ale, which I thoroughly enjoyed.

A painting of Boojum in the dining area overlooks patrons as they eat. It's the only full-body representation of Boojum that can be found at the brewery. It depicts the Boojum as an old mountain man, barefoot with a long, furry tail, carrying a jug. He looks a bit like Gandalf from *The Lord of the Rings*, with a long gray beard and a pointy hat. In the portrait, he's entering his cave, which is filled with jugs. One jug is broken and spills out a multitude of shiny colorful gems.

We spoke with one of the co-owners of Boojum Brewery—the delightful Kelsey Baker—who kindly gave us several minutes of her time to tell us about the business and, most importantly, why Boojum. The brewery is a family business, and Kelsey owns it along with her brother and parents. The family had made plans years before to move to Waynesville and open a brewery. They wanted to give it a name that signified something special and unique to the area. Their real estate agent sent them the story of Boojum, and it immediately clicked.

While looking for someone to talk to about the Boojum, I was given the contact information for Carl Mimms, a self-proclaimed mountain man and landscape photographer. Carl hosts an Instagram page called "Rucksack Living" in which he photographs the beauty of his natural surroundings. I asked Carl if he could tell me about his life and experiences in the wild. He told me he's "a wanderer of the environment, living from my rucksack and photographing along the way, bush-whacking the terrain looking for the out of the ordinary."

I was told by a few Waynesville townsfolk that Carl has made a point of going out in search of the Boojum. I asked him what he could tell me, and he said, "There are two crossings on 215 where Boojum has been seen crossing the road. I have had songbirds block my path calling at me until I stopped all movement. They quit calling. I could feel a heightened sensory effect. Listening and watching, I could hear and see movement in the trees. Once it moved through, the birds flew away. This was in middle-prong wilderness."

Carl claims to have seen the Boojum himself moving through a bear sanctuary on Yellow Gap Road. He insists that everything with his encounter was peaceful, but that he was amazed at how many songbirds blocked his path in the presence of the Boojum. He also referred to multiple beings, perhaps more like other cryptids, such as Bigfoot, just strolling through campgrounds while he sipped his coffee in the stillness of the moment. Carl speaks of a certain mood in the air—the feeling of being in the presence of something unknown, something special.

We've been told that another good location to go to learn more about the Boojum is Lake Logan and the conference center in Canton. We weren't able to make the trip, but apparently there's even Boojum hiking trails. The only other location that has been so closely connected was Eagle Nest Inn, which, as we know, no longer exists. But there is an Eagle Nest Road near Waynesville. Perhaps the secrets to the mystery of the Boojum lie in the woods near Eagle Nest. Traditional thinking would suggest that if the Boojum had lived so long ago, like any creature of the Great Smoky Mountains, it would likely have died off by now. But what about Hootin' Annie, their family, and the hordes of gems Boojum collected over the years? Perhaps one day Carl Mimms will come across Boojum's collection in a cave and post about it—adding to this rich and colorful story.

CHAPTER 3

Helen's Bridge and Chicken Alley

Asheville, North Carolina

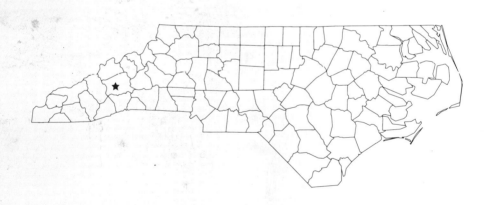

PODCAST • SEASON 2 • EPISODE 8
(December 14, 2018)

The Zealandia Bridge in Asheville, North Carolina, is a beautiful arched stone bridge built in 1909. It was designed by one of the men who worked on the Biltmore Estate. The novelist Thomas Wolfe crossed the bridge often as a young boy and mentioned it in his work *Look Homeward, Angel*. Despite its historic past, the bridge is best known for the dark story that surrounds it. It is known by most as Helen's Bridge.

The story says that a young woman named Helen lived near the Zealandia Estate with her daughter. There was nothing in the world that Helen loved more than her daughter. The estate, and the castle that sat on it, belonged to John Evans Brown, who made a fortune raising sheep in New Zealand. The legend claims that Helen worked at the estate and would sometimes bring her daughter to work with her. Helen caught the eye of John Evans, and they began to have an affair.

One day, while Helen was entertaining Evans, a fire broke out in another part of the castle. When it was brought under control, Helen's daughter was found burned to death. Distraught with guilt and sadness, Helen hanged herself from the Zealandia Bridge.

But the legend doesn't end there.

She is said to appear to motorists as they drive under the bridge. Some claim to have car troubles near the bridge. Most often it's the car's battery going dead; sometimes directly under the bridge, sometimes days afterward.

Helen is also said to wander the grounds around the bridge, in a long, flowing gown, asking people if they have seen her daughter.

Most people claim that Helen means no harm, while others say that the paranormal presence at the bridge isn't Helen at all, but something darker and malevolent in nature. They cite as proof the fact that some people's cars may break down as much as a week after visiting the place.

A few people have reported seeing monsterlike creatures lurking in the dense woods. And some claim to have been scratched and slapped while near the bridge. Apparitions, orbs, and electronic voice phenomena (EVPs) have been documented during paranormal investigations. The Zealandia website urges that no one provoke the spirits around the bridge, since some people have claimed to have been followed home by "something they only see out of the corner of their eye."

As with most of these stories, there are many versions of the legend. Some say that Helen lived in the 1930s, long after John Evans had passed away. Some say she did not work at the estate at all but simply lived nearby. All the versions of the story, however, agree that Helen's daughter died in a fire and that she remains on the grounds today.

Not far from Helen's Bridge is Chicken Alley, a narrow alley in a populated section of downtown Asheville. The name comes from the fact that chickens were frequently sold in the alley during the early days of the city. Today, the only chickens found there are in the large mural by local artist Molly Must. This otherwise forgotten walkway is said to be the home of the ghost of Dr. Jamie Smith.

Dr. Smith was a prominent Asheville physician at the end of the nineteenth century. He was easily spotted, walking the streets with his medicine bag and wearing his unique black, wide-brimmed fedora and long, duster-style coat. And he always carried a cane with him . . . its silver tip clicking on the rough Asheville roads.

In those days, Asheville wasn't the hip, eclectic city it is today; it was a rough logging town. After a hard, dangerous week of working at the nearby logging camps, men would flow into Asheville on the weekend, looking to let off some steam and have a good time. The bars and brothels stayed open late into the night, and Dr. Smith was no stranger to them. The good doctor found the Asheville nightlife not only a source of satisfying personal

entertainment but also a business opportunity; it's said that the bulk of his practice came from treating the various "social diseases" that are often associated with brothels.

Unfortunately, all good things come to an end. For Dr. Smith, this was in 1902, when he decided to walk into the Broadway Tavern located in Chicken Alley for an early drink before visiting a nearby brothel. But Dr. Smith unwittingly entered the tavern in the midst of a huge bar fight. While trying to break up the melee, he was stabbed in the heart and killed instantly. The man responsible was never caught.

A year later, Broadway Tavern burned to the ground.

Some say that the ghost of Dr. Smith burned the place down because, ever since, a peculiar apparition has been seen lurking in Chicken Alley.

He's said to be a shadowy man wearing a long, black coat and a wide-brimmed black hat. He carries an old-fashioned physician's bag and a cane, which can be heard tapping as the figure makes its way down the alley. The figure has been reported for more than a hundred years, and its appearance has stayed remarkably consistent.

DAN'S STORY

I first visited Helen's Bridge in 2010, on my first wedding anniversary (I know, some way to mark the occasion). My poor wife was, and is, such a trouper to put up with me and my interests. She knows that if there's a story attached to a location, especially if it's a spooky or macabre story, that I'm eventually going to pay a visit; not because I want to investigate any kind of haunting, but because there's value for me in the simple act of going to a place and standing there. When I read a book or watch a film or listen to a podcast about a story that took place somewhere real, visiting it gives me a closer connection to that story. It gives me the ability to reminisce about my own experience.

As I write this account about two trips to Helen's Bridge, a decade apart, I can't help but think about this story from my own perspective. A friend of mine who grew up in Asheville told me she used to go there in the middle of the night and stand under the bridge with her friends. When I asked her if she said the three words that supposedly make Helen appear, she looked at me with surprise. She thought only kids from the area were familiar with that particular piece of lore, then she admitted that she was too chicken to try it for herself. So I tried it

in 2010, in the middle of the night, in the cold, as my wife rolled her eyes, sitting back in the car, patiently waiting for me to return. As you might've imagined, that was a fairly uneventful trip. I didn't summon any spirits that night (that I know of), nor was I really trying to. I just couldn't resist the opportunity to stand in the place and say the words myself: Helen, come forth!

Skipping forward to ten years later, as I stood under the bridge once again, in the cold and rainy weather, I was taken aback by the sharp echo of my own voice as I said the words to summon Helen. It's an impressive sound, and not one that was audible unless directly under the bridge itself. Once I got over the initial giddiness of being back there, I began looking the area over and asking questions. It occurred to my research team and me not only that the bridge was fairly old and creepy but that we needed to see the roadway on top of it. We needed to see where it came from and where it led to. So we stood by and watched as sports cars sped around the winding curves of the road and zipped up the steep hill leading to the bridge.

In between bickering over how to pronounce "Beaucatcher," we got back in our car and made our way up Windswept Street, around several sharp curves, and finally found what we were looking for—a big, muddy mess. A small patch of ground that sits behind a guardrail had been reduced to a thick area of mud that was torn up by tire tracks and footprints. We parked our car along the nearby shoulder and made our way up to it on foot. Surprisingly, there was no gate on the chain-link fence leading to the top of the bridge, and there were no signs warning of trespassing. We trekked through the mess and found ourselves on the top of the old and creepy structure.

The first question raised by Sammie was this: "Where did she hang herself from?" Jeff and I had to reaffirm that our interest and subsequent inquiry was not a fact-finding or debunking expedition. Our job is not to confirm or bust any myth but to present the story as it's been told, time and time again, and then to synthesize what it's like to visit—that's how I might've put it. Jeff more bluntly said, "It's a damn story; just go with it." Not to say that there weren't places in which someone might have hanged themselves from on the bridge, but the real-life facts of this story are irrelevant, and the legend might not have been the result of an actual event.

On top of the bridge, it's apparent that time has not been kind. The ground is covered in dirt and grass, trees have grown up around the sides and on the bridge itself, graffiti—which appeared more like colorful chalk markings—was etched along multiple places, and at several places throughout the tops and sides, chunks were missing and gave the impression that perhaps visitors had taken a little piece of Helen's Bridge home with them. If you know anything about famously haunted locations, you'll know that taking a piece home with you is a

very bad idea. This is a common thread in many haunted-house tales. If you decide to go to Helen's Bridge, remember—disturb the site at your own risk.

That's when it hit me—while standing on the bridge, contemplating the very nature of the story—it's a cautionary tale. A story told from friend to friend, neighbor to neighbor, from parent to child, in an effort to ward off anyone from the property who doesn't belong. While standing on the bridge, looking up toward the top of the hill at the obscured, foggy outline of Zealandia Castle, I could easily imagine a group of kids staring up in fear, daring and even double-dog-daring each other just to run up the hill and touch the door. Naturally, when a creepy old place— especially one abandoned and decaying—takes on this role in the community, as the spooky old house on the hill, you can easily see how a ghost story would develop, especially a ghost story specifically surrounding the bridge leading to the house. If you believed the story, then crossing the bridge would be a big risk, maybe even an invitation to dance with the devil in the pale moonlight. Perhaps for local kids, Helen is a cautionary tale about who could "get you" if you were brave enough to wander up Beaucatcher Mountain.

After we had our fill of the bridge, we turned our attention to the object for which the bridge was presumably made—Zealandia. I had reached out to representatives of Zealandia Holding Company in preparation for our trip and was told that it has been renovated and converted into an office space, and, being a place of work and business, that a tour would not be permitted. But once we were there, that didn't stop us from at least snooping around a bit. The driveway that leads to the castle begins painting the picture of an old property, adorned in unusual architecture and landscaping. Stone stairways that lead to mazelike structures and shrubbery give off an Overlook Hotel vibe.

However, in the parking lot, perched at the top of the hill, it's seemingly all business. I approached two friendly ladies leaving the building, presumably headed to their cars, and asked them where we could enter, which they pointed out for us. They said that inside the doorway were brochures providing details about the castle, and that sometimes the receptionist will offer quick "looks around" to curious visitors.

As we entered through the heavy wooden doors, we were immediately struck by its beauty and grandeur. It was easy to imagine from a cursory look around what it might've been like to inhabit such a space in its heyday. The ballroom is adorned with a beautiful mural along the tops of the walls, which seem to tell the story of Zealandia. If you look closely you can even see the inclusion of the bridge itself. Near the entrance is a great hall with a beautiful fireplace and a large wooden staircase. Immediately behind the initial façade is in fact a series of offices. We never encountered any employees who asked us our business.

On the other side of the ballroom, several children were playing and talking, though we could see them only hazily through the glass doors and mused how funny it would be if it turned out there were no children on the premises. We decided not to press our luck and run into hostility. On our way out, we noticed several frames on the wall that displayed black-and-white photographs of parties from one hundred years ago or so, which look like they should feature Jack Torrence at a party, just to further solidify the creepy vibe.

Standing in front of the castle, from the very top of Beaucatcher Mountain, there's a beautiful view of the city. As we looked out at the city of Asheville, obscured in fog and mystery, we couldn't help but wonder why there are so many parallels of ghost stories and bridges. In this book alone, we cover not only Helen's Bridge but Lydia's Bridge in Jamestown and the Bostian Bridge in Statesville. Maybe the key to understanding the ghost story attached to Zealandia is the fact that the tragedy and subsequent haunting are forever tied to the structure that connects the property to the outside world. Perhaps ghosts are bridges themselves between this world and the next.

CHAPTER 4

The Wampus Cat and the Demon Dog

Cherokee, North Carolina
Valle Crucis, North Carolina

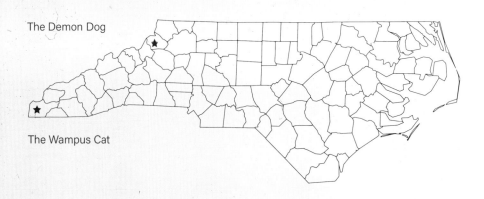

The Demon Dog

The Wampus Cat

PODCAST • SEASON 2 • EPISODE 2
(October 5, 2018)

The Appalachian Mountain Range runs along the North Carolina–Tennessee border, but the two states share more than just rolling, misty peaks. A catlike beast is said to roam this area. It's described as a howling, evil creature with glowing eyes of yellow that pierces men's hearts, driving them into insanity. And it walks upright, like a human.

The Cherokee believed it was a demon named Ewah. Some know it as Gallywampus. Others call it the Whistling Wampus. But it is most commonly known as the Wampus Cat of the Appalachians. Legend has it that the beast can transform into a woman and has been seen as a combination of half woman, half cat; no, not like Catwoman. The creature has been reported as far back as two hundred years ago and, the lore says, is cursed to wander the Appalachian hills for eternity.

According to the full legend, the Wampus Cat was once a beautiful Cherokee woman who did not trust her husband. He would often go on very long hunting trips with some of the other tribesmen. She was convinced that he was having an affair, and finally, one day, she followed them into the woods. It was forbidden for the women to participate in the tribe's hunts in any way, so she covered herself with the pelt of a mountain lion.

When the men stopped for the night, they built a campfire and settled in around it. They each told stories of the great hunts and performed powerful magic rites. The woman hid nearby and listened to their tales. Now, if a woman being in the woods with the men during a hunt was forbidden, for a woman to witness the tribe's secret magic rituals was extremely taboo.

She was discovered and brought before the group of warriors. The elders allowed the woman to stand witness to one last piece of tribal magic. They cast a remarkably powerful spell . . . on her!

The mountain lion hide that she was wearing slowly began to spread and bond with her own flesh, her teeth lengthened into fangs, her face became more catlike, and she grew a long, furry tail. She became the Wampus Cat.

Maybe that's why so many hunters and campers have reported being stalked through the forests of the Appalachians. Of course, there's no shortage of fearsome creatures in those hills, from the common bear to Bigfoot, but these reports are different. These folks claim to see a giant cat—like the group of campers who were reportedly attacked while in the Virginia section of the Blue Ridge Parkway. One of the men claimed they were besieged by "a thing . . . definitely not a primate . . . no Bigfoot or anything . . . and not a bear." One man continued, "I swear we were almost killed by a walking cat!"

Another story tells of a poacher who went out hunting one night. As he neared a bend in the trail, his dogs got spooked and ran off into the woods. As the man turned the corner, he was overcome by a horrible stench like a mix between a skunk and a wet dog. But that was nothing compared to the shock when he found himself staring face to face with the Wampus! He said it was as big as a panther but walked upright. He claimed its eyes glowed orange in the dark of night.

As you may expect, all intentions of poaching drained from his thoughts as quickly as the color did from his face. He dropped the gun and ran as fast as he could—foolish, perhaps, but none of us can deny that most primal of responses: fight or flight. As he sprinted down the path, he could hear the creature gaining on him. He realized that there was no way he could make it back home. There was no place to go. He was deep in the woods. Then he saw a small, abandoned hunter's cabin. He made a desperate dash to the door. He threw the bolt just as the creature slammed into the other side. Surprisingly, the old door held up. The man spent the rest of the night sitting against the wall, hugging his knees, and listening to the beast pace relentlessly around the cabin.

Finally, the first light of dawn cracked over the horizon. The Wampus Cat let out an ear-piercing shriek and ran off into the trees.

These days, sightings of the Wampus Cat are few and far between, and many people just chalk it up to yet another fictitious myth of the North Carolina mountains. But those who have seen the mysterious beast know it to be a horrifying reality, still stalking the Appalachian Mountains, hunting for its next victim.

On the other end of western North Carolina sits Valle Crucis, a small, quiet mountain community located on Highway 194. Its name means "Valley of the Cross," and two nearby streams cross at almost right angles in the valley where Valle Crucis lies. They form the rough shape of a cross.

Valle Crucis is home to the first Mast General Store and is also home to St. John the Baptist Episcopal Church. Reverend William West Skiles founded Valle Crucis and built St. John's in the 1840s. Accessible by just an old dirt road, the small, wooden church sits isolated on a lonely ridge with an ancient, weathered cemetery as its front yard. St. John's lost its congregation years ago, and now the nearby Church of the Holy Cross cares for the old building. It's used only for special services and to house the ghosts that reside there.

Popular legend claims that a new, young priest came to St. John's with ideas for growing the small church. But instead, the congregation slowly dwindled to nothing. Distraught over his failure, the heartbroken priest hanged himself from the bell tower.

It seems this story is completely bogus, though. There are no records of a new priest ever coming to St. John's, and no record of a suicide within its walls. Rev. Skiles passed away of natural causes in 1862 and lies buried in the graveyard outside the church.

But just because the story isn't true doesn't mean there isn't a ghost at St. John's. Too many people have seen and heard things that can't be explained. Tapping noises and footsteps have been heard, and mysterious lights witnessed. A group of Appalachian State students ran from the building when all their flashlights went out simultaneously.

Michael Renegar tells the story of Mitch and Rhonda, who parked near the church for some . . . privacy. Just as Mitch was about to kiss Rhonda, she jerked away and whispered, "There's a man watching us." Mitch looked and saw a man, backlit from the light inside the church. He wore a black hat

and long garments. Mitch couldn't see the man's face but could tell that he was not happy the two lovers had parked so close to the church.

Over Rhonda's protests, Mitch decided to go apologize to the man, who he assumed was a priest from the Church of the Holy Cross. The church's door was unlocked and the lights were still on when Mitch entered the church, but he didn't see anyone else there.

"Hello?" he called as he made his way down to the pulpit of the small church. "I just wanted to say sorry."

But no one answered.

Where could the man have gone? The church isn't that big, and the door was unlocked with the lights on. Just then, a chill wind swirled around Mitch and he screamed his apology to thin air as he ran from the building. As they drove away, he looked in his rearview mirror and noticed that the lights were now off inside the building.

A female apparition has also been reported in the area, as well as unexplained gunshots and the sound of a woman crying.

If you go looking for the ghosts of St. John's, beware. Something else lurks in the misty shadows of Valle Crucis.

The story goes that two men were driving past St. John's Church on a clear, autumn night when a shadow leapt from behind one of the graves and crossed the road in front of them. The driver slammed on the brakes to avoid it, and when they stopped, the men were staring at a dog—a big damned dog.

It was as tall and wide as a full-grown man and was described as part Rottweiler, part bear. Its black fur bristled as the animal snarled, baring its sharp, yellow teeth at the car, but what really terrified the men were the beast's eyes. They glowed red in the dark night, as if lit by the very fires of hell.

"Do you see that?" the driver asked.

"No," said his friend, "and neither do you."

The dog began to slowly stalk toward the car, and the driver immediately slammed his foot down on the gas. They raced down the mountain roads, skittering around each corner.

The man in the passenger seat put his arm on the driver's shoulder and turned to tell him to slow down, that they were safe now—but as he turned, he saw that the beast was running after them . . . and it was gaining.

Finally, the car crossed the bridge where the two streams meet, and the dog slid to a stop; unwilling, it seemed, to cross the water.

This wasn't an isolated incident; several people have reported seeing the beast. Some call it the Hellhound, while others say it is the Broadstone Hound, but most know it as . . .

The Demon Dog of Valle Crucis.

DAN'S STORY

While planning our trip to Valle Crucis to visit St. John's Episcopal Church, we considered trying to visit during a service; however, considering the building was dedicated in 1862, it's quite old-fashioned and used only for special services by another congregation. In any case, it seemed perhaps more appropriate to arrive in the middle of the night to experience a bit of fright ourselves, much like others who have lived to tell the tale.

Our trip was made on a cold, rainy night—perfect conditions to visit a haunted place, right? Not exactly. I can't speak for my companions, but I had plenty of fear as my two-wheel-drive vehicle slid from side to side, struggling to get up a gravel road at what seemed to be an impossible angle. To make matters worse, the church wasn't exactly where we had planned on it being, and neither of us had cell phone service to look things up. After very nearly getting stuck—or worse, sliding down the side of the mountain—we decided to drive back to town.

That's when Sammie pointed out a side road and suggested we take it. At that point, we didn't have anything to lose, and driving on a paved road didn't seem like such a bad thing. Shortly after taking the turn, our fears were allayed as we crept up on the tall, white, spectral-looking image of the church on a hill.

Relief washed over us as we buttoned up our coats and entered the property for a closer look. We're always very mindful about potentially trespassing or violating privacy when visiting these locations, but there was no posted "Trespassing" sign on the grounds, and we didn't have to climb a fence or open a gate to simply walk onto the grounds; however, I noted on our way in a posted sign that read:

"Playing on tombstones can be dangerous

Please respect our hallowed ground

Children must be supervised

Recorded video monitoring"

Sammie pointed out that there was a glowing red light on inside the building. My heart skipped a beat as I was immediately reminded of the legends in which visitors recall seeing lights on inside. I reminded everyone else of the legend, and as you might expect, we all hurried our pace along the path.

Our next question was whether or not the church was currently in use, because the ground had been so well kept. Despite the building's age, it looked to be in remarkably good shape. The roof seemed to be brand new. The presence of picnic tables nearby gave the impression that this was a commonly used place. We briefly explored the grounds outside the church house and the adjoining graveyard. I noted the presence of an outhouse directly behind the building, and it didn't appear to be there as a joke.

Upon settling in one spot in the graveyard and turning off our lights, we were immediately struck by the overwhelming darkness of the place. Given that it was raining, there were too many clouds to even see moonlight or stars. While we stood still in the dark, taking in our environment, a member of our group saw something strange.

Chad couldn't help but ask, "Did you see that red light down there by the tombstones?" His question provoked no immediate response other than silence as we all turned to look where he was pointing. He added, "That one that says Booth right there, there was just a red light, like a . . ."

Being as familiar with the legends as anyone, Jeff interrupted in his matter-of-fact style, "Well, if you see two of them, that's the demon dog's eyes."

Not joking around, Chad continued to explain, "I only saw one, and it was a pinpoint light, like a laser pointer or something." Jeff then confessed, "I thought I saw that a couple of times, but I wasn't sure."

"I just saw it right there," Chad said while pointing directly to a tombstone.

I chalked it up to our eyes adjusting to the darkness. It also occurred to me that perhaps Chad was simply thinking about the story of the Demon Dog and was allowing his imagination to play tricks on him. The more we talked about it, though, it turned out that Chad hadn't heard our episode on the Demon Dog yet and wasn't familiar with the story prior to our visit.

I told Chad it was likely our aging eyes struggling to adjust to the sudden change in light. Always the smart ass, Chad responded, "I don't know." After a pause, he continued, "But it's pretty nice of you to try to explain it away to help my feelings."

I then reminded the group that part of the Demon Dog legend is that it growls and chases you with its glowing red eyes. It's more than just seeing the eyes, or one eye.

After another moment of silence and stillness, just taking in the creepy surroundings, Sammie informed me that he was hearing something walking in the nearby wood line.

I then hit the area with my high-powered flashlight and didn't see a thing. "It's probably just a deer or something," he added. After we returned to darkness, he let us know that he continued hearing the sound of something walking among the trees. Sammie provided the only needed explanation with "Huh, well it's a creepy old place." I agreed.

During our short visit with the church and graveyard, we were freezing our asses off. As you can imagine, in February, in Valle Crucis, the weather was somewhere in between a light drizzle and full-on rain. While we were attempting to find the place, it had been sleeting quite heavily. An hour or so before that, it had been snowing. Not enough for accumulation, but enough to slow down the commute.

As we approached the side of the church to get a look in the windows, we didn't see anyone looking back at us, thank God. The inside appeared to be a very basic structure with heavy wood paneling. It's an old country church, like many erected in North Carolina during the period; however, one modern convenience stood out and was the source of our mysterious red light, noted upon arrival. The state-mandated "Exit" sign glowed a bright red in the dark, lighting up an entire section of the church. It was the only illumination coming from within.

We knew better than to start pulling on doors to gain entry to the building. Not only would that be trespassing, perhaps breaking and entering, but it would simply be disrespectful to the current property managers and to the potential spirits that dwell within. We could get a close enough look from the outside, and besides, we didn't exactly get a welcoming vibe from the place.

After approximately ten minutes, this visit was certainly the briefest of our trips, despite the several-hour drive between destinations. As we all got back in the car, a bit relieved to get back in some warmth, I couldn't help but check out the graveyard with my flashlight to make sure we weren't being followed. I can't say that I saw any glowing red eyes in my rearview mirror, but you can rest assured that I checked.

CHAPTER 5

The Moon-Eyed People

Murphy, North Carolina

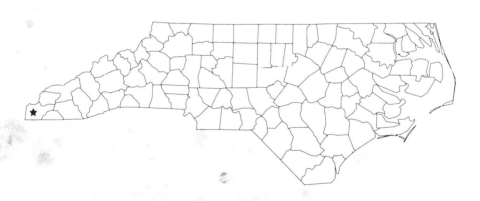

PODCAST • SEASON 3 • EPISODE 14
(March 13, 2020)

Indian folklore is rich with mythology and mysterious legends. It's easy to think that the Cherokee were the first inhabitants of western North Carolina, but according to their own history they migrated to the area about a thousand years ago. When they did, they claimed there were already a group of people living in the area whom the Cherokee referred to as the Moon-Eyed People.

The Indians describe them as short, pale, and having very blue eyes. They lived underground and were ultrasensitive to light, so they ventured out only in the darkest night. Even a full moon was too much light for their eyes to handle.

The Cherokee noticed that the Moon-Eyed People stayed on one particular side of the river, so the Cherokee made their camp on the *other* side of the river, very close to the junction of the Hiwassee and the Valley Rivers, in what we know today as Murphy. The Cherokee people found a spot where the rocks formed a natural ridge, perfect for crossing the river. The Moon-Eyed People were too scared to cross the river and warned the Cherokee that they shouldn't ever cross it either—they each must stay on their own sides.

Eventually the Cherokee "forcefully displaced" the Moon-Eyed People. Soon afterward they discovered the meaning behind the Moon-Eyed People's warning. One day they saw a giant red . . . *thing* lying in the river below the ridge. It was as big as a house, and as they watched it, it unfurled. It was a giant leech with red and white stripes! Then it slithered down into a deep, deep pool.

Thinking that it was now safe to cross the river, several braves ventured across the ridge, but as they did, the river began to boil and foam and a great wave of water rose up and swept the men into the river below. Later, the bodies were found downstream, with their ears and noses missing. Eventually the Cherokee treated the Giant Red Leech as a sort of rite of passage. They held ceremonies where select members would *brave* the ridge crossing to prove their courage and fortitude.

The only known depiction of the Moon-Eyed People is a statue that was found when the Europeans settled in Murphy, North Carolina. It now resides in the Cherokee County Historical Museum in downtown Murphy. The statue is made of soapstone, just like Judaculla Rock, and stands about 3 feet tall. There isn't a lot of detail to the carving; it simply depicts two Moon-Eyed People joined along the torso. One figure is slightly larger than the other. The faces are flat and highlighted by two large, round eyes.

Even though the Moon-Eyed People were described as "short," it doesn't necessarily mean they were a 3-foot, hobbit-sized race. They may have merely been shorter than the Cherokee people. Cherokee County historian Billy Ray Palmer surmises that the statue was made shorter out of convenience—it would have been a lot easier to carve the figures at 3 feet rather than 6 feet, and, who knows, maybe everyone is simply overthinking it. Perhaps the statue is 3 feet tall because that was simply the size of the original rock they decided to work with. He also proposes the possibility that the statue may represent the two rivers that run through Murphy, the Hiwassee River and the slightly smaller Valley River. Remember, one of the figures is slightly smaller than the other, and it was found on the lot of land right in the confluence of the two rivers, so it makes for a fairly plausible theory; however, there is no denying that a race of people *were* in residence in the Appalachians before the Cherokee arrived.

Ultimately, the Cherokee forced the Moon-Eyed People out of the area. Taking full advantage of the Moon-Eyed People's weaknesses, the Cherokee attacked them during the full moon, when their adversary couldn't see well enough to defend themselves.

According to a marker displayed at Fort Mountain by the Georgia State Parks & Historic Sites, the Delaware Indians also had run-ins with other Moon-Eyed People they called the Allegewi along the Ohio and the Mississippi Rivers. The Allegewi were recorded as being tall with light skin, light hair, and gray eyes. They were also said to carry strange weapons and tools.

The Moon-Eyed People are mentioned in numerous eighteenth-century manuscripts and books. Colonel Leonard Marbury, an early settler of Georgia, said that the little folk were called "Moon-Eyed People" because they saw poorly during the day. Barton put forth his own theory as to their origin, suggesting that perhaps they were the descendants of the albino Kuna people of Panama, who were also called moon-eyed due to their trouble with daylight.

Time and time again, the Moon-Eyed People are mentioned in Cherokee lore and are credited with having built ancient rock structures and mounds in the region—including the impressive 885-foot-long wall that gives Fort Mountain its name. Built in the traditional Welsh style, the structure zigzags across the peak of the mountain, dividing the north peak from the southern side of the mountain. In 1810, Tennessee governor John Sevier wrote in a letter that Cherokee chief Oconostota told him in a conversation decades prior of the race of white people who built the mounds and were subsequently pushed off the land by his elders.

One theory suggests that the Moon-Eyed People were likely part of the Adena people from Ohio, who migrated and eventually integrated with the Cherokee. To complicate things further, throughout history they were also

referred to as "Welsh Indians." Some accounts say that the Cherokee found the Moon-Eyed People to speak with a strange Welsh dialect.

In 1804, in a letter to Meriwether Lewis, President Thomas Jefferson wrote of searching for the Welsh Indians, who were said to now be in Missouri. According to the book *Undaunted Courage* by Stephen E. Ambrose, about the Lewis and Clarke expedition, President Jefferson was a believer in the Madoc theory and asked the expedition to search for the Welsh Indians. History also references them as the Monacan people or the Mandan people. Numerous tribes have been said to be descendants of the Mandan, but typically the term "Welsh Indian" has been associated with Mandan.

So, you may be wonder, What's Madoc? And how do the Welsh fit into this? Many people think that the Moon-Eyed People were a lost colony of Welsh settlers. The tale goes like this:

Prince Madoc (or Madog in some stories) was the son of King Owen Gwyneth, the ruler of northern Wales. In the year 1169, King Gwyneth died. His thirteen children and close relatives met to discuss the land and succession of power. The discussions quickly turned bloody. Prince Madoc was said to be a peace-loving man and didn't want any part of the quarrel. In order to avoid the war and to take his name out of consideration, it's said he embarked on a journey westward to reach the ends of the earth. In some versions of the story, he's accompanied by his brother, Prince Rhirid. The story goes that they set off across the Atlantic and, after several weeks, landed somewhere in what is now known as Mobile Bay, Alabama.

After some exploration, they decided to establish a permanent colony. Rhirid stayed behind while Madoc sailed back to Wales to recruit ambitious settlers. He managed to fill ten ships with Welsh families eager for a fresh start in the New World. None of them were ever heard from again. There is a large segment of folks who believe Madoc, Rhirid, and the Welsh mated with local Indians and spread through Alabama, Florida, Georgia, and finally North Carolina.

The tale of Madoc is a fascinating legend on its own, coming from medieval tradition about a Welsh hero and brave sea voyager. Some historians suggest that it was used as a legal justification in the Elizabethan era to assert prior discovery of the Americas by England before Spain. Many believe now that Madoc himself was a lie, fabricated by the Crown to establish this justification. There's not exactly any record of King Gwyneth having a son named Madoc, and there certainly aren't any records from the New World; however, in 1953 a plaque was displayed on the shores of Mobile Bay by the Daughters of the American Revolution, which read: "In memory of Prince Madoc, a Welsh explorer who landed on the shores of Mobile Bay in 1170 and left behind with the Indians the Welsh language." The historical marker was removed by the state parks service in 2008.

Whether you believe in Prince Madoc or not, here's where things get even weirder. The rock formations found in the Appalachians *are* built in the Welsh style, and there were quite a few seventeenth-century stories about explorers encountering Welsh-speaking Indians. There's even a roadside plaque at Fort Mountain crediting the construction of their ancient wall to Prince Madoc.

Our producing partner, Sammie Cassell, wears a piece of staurolite on a chain around his neck. It's a stone that naturally formed in the shape of a cross. He wears it as a reminder of where he came from—Patrick County, Virginia. It's one of just a handful of places in the world where you can find the rock, also known as fairy stones. Patrick County is even home to Fairy Stone State Park.

Another place where fairy stones can be found is Cherokee County, North Carolina. There are quite a few legends surrounding fairy stones, including how they got their name. Some say that they formed in the peculiar shape from the tears of fairies, ancient mythical pixies that used to inhabit the earth; however, folks in Murphy say that the tears were shed at the moment of Christ's crucifixion by none other than . . . the Moon-Eyed People.

Sammie accompanied us along with Chad Hunt on a research trip to the Cherokee County Historical Museum. We got to take a close-up look at some beautiful fairy stones on display, and we also got to take a look at the effigy of the Moon-Eyed People. The statue was found in the mid-1800s by a farmer near Murphy, who was plowing his field. He dug it up and set it aside, not really knowing what he had found. It stayed in private hands for decades until it was finally put on display at the museum in 2015.

DAN'S STORY

Few stories covered on *Carolina Haints* have sparked my imagination like that of the Moon-Eyed People (MEP). It's not so much a story as it is just a concept. And yet, it's intriguing and fills my overactive brain with all kinds of ideas. The more I learn about this topic, the more questions I have. It's caused me to lose hours of my life burrowing deeper and deeper down the YouTube rabbit holes exploring Prince Madoc, genetic mutations, Cherokee folklore, and even conspiracy theories. Yes, one theory suggests that President Jefferson sent

Lewis and Clarke out west to hunt down the MEP, since they were a potential threat to US sovereignty.

The questions regarding the Moon-Eyed People don't seem to have any sort of satisfying answer; just theories. Questions such as these are asked: Why would the Cherokee run them off the land and not try to peacefully cohabit the area? How did they even converse with the Cherokee? If they lived underground, how did they survive? Where did they go after leaving the area? Did one group attempt to learn the language of the other? Why isn't there more found in written history about the "Welsh Indians"? I mean, if it was well known enough for a president to mention it in writing, wouldn't it have been found more often in the written record? How did Jefferson know about them? Was it just common knowledge?

I have a theory about the MEP that I haven't seen too much of in my research, and it goes along with the assumption that they are descendants of the Welsh explorers from the twelfth century—and that theory involves inbreeding. Despite researching the topic of genetic mutations and homozygous recessive and dominant genes, I'm not going to pretend that I understand all of that. My undergraduate and graduate studies were entirely in the social sciences, so trust me when I say I'm totally unequipped to synthesize these ideas; however, I will say it seems that many of the character traits of the common MEP descriptions are also commonly found through inbreeding. The short body stature, the odd shape of the facial structure, the painfully light eye color—all suggests genetic mutation. Hell, let's not forget the statue itself is of conjoined twins.

Another theory you don't hear about too much in MEP research is perhaps the most obvious one—at least to me. I can't look at the statue without thinking of aliens. Is it just me, or does the statue look like little gray men from outer space? Even the soapstone it's carved from elicits the image of two grays. It's not just the faces with the large eyes, flat faces, and small mouths; it's their large, bald heads and short little bodies. There's also the fact that they come out only at night—have you ever heard of an abduction scenario in the daytime? Perhaps this would play nicely into the Chariot of the Gods type of theories out there. I don't know if MEP have ever been covered on an episode of *Ancient Aliens*, but I can only imagine the rampant conjecture it might evoke.

In any case, back on Earth, the research team and I were fortunate enough to meet with local Cherokee historian Billy Ray Palmer, who talked to us about the Moon-Eyed People and answered every question we had. Billy is a wealth of knowledge on the subject and can even tell you where they think the Big Red Leech was located and subsequently where the MEP may have lived. Billy said he thought the Cherokee created the statue to preserve some sort of record

for future generations about the people they displaced. He also thinks the statue is a representation of the joining of the Valley River and the larger Hiwassee River, but he believes it also may be representative of the Cherokee and MEP joining together. Billy was very patient and generous with his time, and I'd like to thank him once again for his contribution.

I absolutely love this story, and, believe me, we're only scratching the surface. If you ever have the opportunity, I recommend visiting the Cherokee County Historical Museum and seeing the statue for yourself in person. While you're there, check out the Cherokee dance masks and their fairy stone collection. If you're anything like me, you'll get a thrill just in seeing the statue of the Moon-Eyed People in person. Take it in and let your imagination run wild with possibilities. This is such a fascinating and multilayered story with so many deeply rooted facets that we could expand this chapter into a full book.

Who knows? Someday we just might.

CHAPTER 6

Judaculla Rock

Cullowhee, North Carolina

PODCAST • SEASON 4 • EPISODE 13
(March 12, 2021)

Today the Cherokee nation is associated with North Carolina and the Southeast. But the truth is, they're not exactly native to the area. They migrated here from Lake Erie about a thousand years ago, but they weren't even the first "beings" to settle in this region. The others don't sound quite . . . human. It's easy to be skeptical of the creatures that the Cherokee described until you realize they may have left evidence behind.

There's a large soapstone boulder near Cullowhee, a few miles east of Western Carolina University. One side of the rock is relatively flat and sticks up out of the ground at a 45-degree angle. This flat edge alone is around 230 square feet, but the unusual feature about this particular rock is that it's covered with more than 1,500 carvings and pictographs. It's known as Judaculla Rock.

Many people have tried to decipher the message written on the rock, but it's in a long-forgotten tongue. One anthropologist suggested that the rock told the story of the 1775 battle fought between the Cherokee and the Creek Nations, but this theory has some flaws. Maybe you've already guessed it; the stone isn't written in the Cherokee language. Other so-called experts say it could have been created by cavemen at the end of the last ice age. So, we've managed to narrow it down to between two hundred and twelve thousand years old.

The vast majority of the markings in the rock are cup marks—like someone took a tiny ice cream scooper and dished out 1,500 scoops. The rock is also crisscrossed with long, grooved lines. In addition, there are crosses, wavy lines, concentric circles, and some symbols and figures. Some of these figures are open to interpretation; where some may see a fish, others claim to see an owl. But there's relatively no ambiguity to the dominating pictograph: a large, seven-fingered handprint.

The original landowners said that at one time there were three such boulders sitting in this Jackson County field. One was destroyed during a mining operation, and the other has been lost. No one is quite sure if the third rock was buried or removed or simply overgrown with vegetation.

Even though the Cherokee could not read the language of Judaculla Rock, they developed their own legend to explain it. You see, the Cherokee believe that everything has a spirit—humans, animals, the trees, the sky, everything. They believe that a hierarchy of lesser gods, ruled over by the Great Being, look over these spirits. The Cherokee consider the death of the physical body to be trivial. Don't get me wrong; that doesn't mean that they do not grieve the loss of their loved ones, but they believe that nothing really ceases to exist as long as its spirit lives on. To help guard against the true death, the death of the spirit, they believe in a mediator that helps guide their spirits

to the heavens. The Cherokee's spiritual mediator does not have a name because she lived in a time before names. The Cherokee believe that Judaculla Rock is a memorial of the Cherokee's union with the spirit world.

As the story goes . . .

A brave Cherokee warrior was killed in battle, leaving behind a widow, a son, and a daughter. The son was also a fierce warrior, so the family was treated as heroes during times of war; however, the son was a very poor hunter. Through the peaceful years, the family lived on handouts from the other villagers. It was quite literally feast or famine.

One day the warrior's daughter went for a walk near their home on Balsam Mountain. She followed a stream and soon found herself in a beautiful glen. The small clearing had a floor of thick, soft moss, and it was surrounded by laurels and azaleas and rhododendrons. The fragrant flowers combined with the babbling brook put her in a relaxed state. She couldn't help herself; she lay down and fell asleep.

Only then did she realize why the glen seemed so perfect: it was a magical, enchanted place. By falling asleep here, she entered the spirit world. Suddenly, a male spirit appeared. He was strong and handsome and graceful, and when he whispered in her ear, she found herself longing for him. When she realized the spirit was trying to seduce her, she told him to stop.

This pleased the spirit. Never before had anyone resisted his invitation. He immediately proposed marriage. Startled, she could only think to ask if he was a good hunter. She explained that her brother was a mighty warrior but a poor hunter, and her mother would never allow her to marry someone who wasn't a good hunter.

The spirit laughed, for as fate would have it, he was the Spirit of the God of the Hunt. Upon hearing this, the girl gave herself to the spirit and they were wed. Her physical, sleeping body disappeared, and she remained part of the spirit world. The Cherokee say that "the gentle breeze of the spirit world caressed her from that day forward."

Meanwhile, back in the girl's village, her mother and brother grew increasingly alarmed at her disappearance. They were convinced that another tribe had kidnapped her. Together they rallied the village, and soon the brother was leading raiding parties against nearby tribes to search for her.

Of course, they didn't find any trace of her, but the girl saw what was happening from her place in the spirit world. She felt bad that so much blood was being spilled in her name, so she asked her new husband to intervene. He sent a large stag to the girl's family. The deer found the mother and brother and told them that if they wanted to see the girl, they would have to stop the violence and follow it into the woods.

They did.

It led them to a place where a stream ran into a huge boulder, splitting into two streams. On the far side of the stream was a small clearing bordered by the mountain itself. In this area, the mountain rose in a nearly sheer rock face. The stag told them to stay in the space between the stream and the cliff and to fast for seven days.

On the sixth day they heard the beat of a drum, and a cave appeared before them in the rock wall of the mountain. The brother was very hungry and wondered if this was a sign that their fasting was over. He asked the stag, but it only repeated its previous message: fast for seven days. Throughout the day the drumming grew louder. As the sun fell on the sixth day, it was obvious that more than one drum was being sounded. During the night the cave was suddenly lit up by a campfire within.

They had been told to stay in the clearing, so they stood at the mouth of the cave and looked inside. They saw many spirits dancing around the campfire. They were all beautiful and graceful, and the girl was one of them!

On the morning of the seventh day, they were permitted to enter the cave. The brother, now starving, took this as a sign that the fasting was over. He pulled out a piece of dried meat. His mother screamed for him to stop, but it was too late; he greedily shoved it into his mouth. The drums immediately stopped, and they were dispelled from the cave. The campfire was extinguished, and as it went out, the cave vanished as well. The stag sniffed the air and then bolted in fear into the woods.

The Spirit of the God of the Hunt was a spirit that was very quick to anger, and the brother's disobedience greatly angered him. In a deafening clap of thunder, he appeared before them on top of the huge boulder in the fork of the stream. He took the form of Judaculla, a great slant-eyed giant so ugly that men would run from the mere sight of him. He is also said to have seven fingers and seven toes. Judaculla screamed and roared and, they say, lightning bolts flew from his hands.

The girl's mother and brother ran for their lives. They rushed back to the village, where everyone gathered to hear what had happened. The two caught their breath and then told them about the cave and the girl, and about Judaculla. Then the brother gathered the bravest of the village's warriors and led them back to the spot. Along the way, the brother, egged on by the other warriors, worked himself into a rage. His sister was alive. And this big, ugly, slant-eyed giant was keeping him from seeing her. For all he knew, she was being held against her will.

When they arrived in the clearing, there was no sign of the cave or the stag or Judaculla. There was just a fork in the stream and a huge boulder. The brother, still angry, cried out and challenged the spirit. Now, as you may imagine, that didn't go over well. When Judaculla reappeared, his wrath had not diminished.

The other warriors hesitated when Judaculla showed up. They were not stunned by his anger but rather his unimaginable ugliness. Even though the brother had tried to describe the giant, no human words could do his hideousness complete justice.

Once again, the giant threw lightning from his hands and caused the ground to tremble. The brother, however, was unfazed and repeated his challenge. He raised his war club over his head and screamed his best war cry. His cry was cut short by one of Judaculla's lightning bolts as it bore straight through his chest.

Judaculla then sent several bolts over the warriors' heads in warning. A warning that they obeyed. They too ran all the way back to the village so they could tell the widow, who had recently lost her daughter, that her son was now dead as well. The village shaman berated these supposedly brave warriors for their cowardice and ordered them to go back and retrieve the body; in fact, he would go with them.

The mother went with them. She had lost both of her children at that cursed clearing. She intended to pray for them there, and if Judaculla didn't like that, he was welcome to strike her down too and end her suffering.

Meanwhile, the girl was also grieving, both for her brother and for her mother's broken heart. The Spirit of the God of the Hunt tried to apologize for his quick temper, but the girl said that she was going to leave the spirit world. When her mother arrived, she planned to go back home with her. The spirit begged her to stay, but she would not be swayed. Then he offered to become the guardian spirit of the Cherokee. He promised her that he would provide a place for anyone who demonstrated the strength of their heart.

The girl was moved by the offer, which would benefit all the generations of Cherokee to come. While the girl thought over his proposal, the Spirit of the God of the Hunt allowed the spirit of the girl's brother to join them. She was overjoyed and immediately agreed to stay with Judaculla.

When the Cherokee party arrived at the clearing, they found the brother's physical body lying on the huge boulder, which was now inscribed with many intricate marks and carvings. As the shaman studied the rock, the large stag returned and told him that the markings were a guide to the way into the spirit world.

It is said that if one comes to Judaculla Rock . . . and is strong of heart . . . and fasts for seven days, that they will be able to understand the message written in the stone. From that day forth, the Cherokee have occasionally claimed to see the mediator spirit of the girl.

Now, the obvious problem with this story is the fact that Judaculla Rock isn't located in the fork of a stream or near a sheer rock wall.

But there is another story that is also told involving the widow and her two children. In this version, the mother and the girl lived in Kanuga, an old Cherokee town that used to be near Waynesville. The brother had married and moved to another town to start his own family.

The mother and the girl had a small homestead with a house and an asi (what we would call a sweat lodge). When the weather was nice, the girl liked to sleep in the asi. One night, Judaculla came to the girl, disguised as a stranger. He woke her and told her that he wished to marry her. The girl told him that her mother would allow her to marry only a great hunter. He assured her that he was a hunter, so she let him stay the night.

A little before sunrise, the stranger said that he had to leave, but he had left some deer meat for her and her mother. Once the sun rose, the girl went outside and found the meat. She took it to her mother, who was very happy. The following night Judaculla returned. Again, he left before dawn, but this time he had left two whole deer. This time the mother complained that he had not left any firewood as well.

Judaculla, now miles away, heard the mother's complaints, and on the third night he told the girl that he had brought them some wood. The following morning the women found a deer draped over three large trees. Of course, the mother then complained that they did not have the means to cut up all this wood.

Night after night, Judaculla visited the girl, and each morning the girl and her mother found a gift of either deer or some other type of game, but he never again left them with any wood. Sometimes the giant left more meat than the mother and the girl could eat, and they shared the excess with the other villagers. The mother grew curious about her daughter's nightly visitor. He always came after sunset and left before the sun rose. The mother had never seen Judaculla and asked to do so.

The girl relayed this message on Judaculla's next visit, and he explained that it would frighten her mother to see him. The girl cried and begged him until he finally conceded.

"But she must not say anything about my appearance," he warned.

The next morning, Judaculla stayed in the asi and did not leave as usual. The girl brought her mother in, and what did she see? The most hideous beast she had ever laid eyes on! And he was so large that he had to double up to fit inside the asi. His feet were up in the rafters on one side, and his head was squished against the wall on the opposite side. The girl's mother ran away screaming. This angered the giant. He declared that neither the girl nor her mother would ever see him again. He left for his home, a large cave near Tanasee Bald on Balsam Mountain.

The girl was upset, and since they had been together for several nights, she suspected that she was with child, but then she got her period. At first she was relieved, but that quickly turned to panic. There was a lot of blood ... too much. Her mother gathered it by the bucketful and threw it into the river. Finally, the bleeding stopped and things returned to normal.

Soon after this, Judaculla came to the girl late one night and asked where the child was.

"There is no child," the girl said.

Judaculla asked if she had bled, and when she said she had, he asked where the blood was. Hearing that her mother had thrown it into the river upset him greatly. He demanded to know exactly where the blood was discarded. She took him to the spot, and he reached down in the water and pulled out a small worm.

The giant carefully cradled the worm, and by the time they got back to the girl's house, it had grown into a newborn baby girl. Judaculla was not happy with the girl's mother. He said that not only had her mother insulted him, but she had also abused their child. He swore to never return to their home again. The girl asked if she could go with him, and together they returned to Tanasee Bald. As a sort of tribute, Judaculla left several deer for the mother. There was enough meat for the entire village of Kanuga to feast that night, but the mother was too angry to enjoy the celebration. Her daughter had abandoned her.

Soon after this, the girl's brother came to visit with them and found his mother weeping. She told him the girl had abandoned her and left with the giant. The brother decided to track down Judaculla and ask the girl to return home. He had no trouble tracking them, because the giant left . . . well . . . giant tracks. They also left clear signs at each of the places where they stopped to rest.

At the first place they rested, the brother found signs of another child being born. He also found a huge rock where the worm had been allowed to crawl around. According to this version of the legend, the markings on Judaculla Rock are from the path of the worm as it played on the stone.

The brother continued on, and at the second resting place he found signs of two children, one walking and one crawling. At the third spot, one child was running and the other walking. So it went until he reached a steep slope on Tanasee Bald. The climb was difficult, and he was almost ready to turn back, when he found a small ledge. The ledge led him to a cave entrance, and he found himself inside a huge meeting room. Several other tunnels led off in other directions, but they were all pitch dark. The meeting chamber was lit by a campfire, and he saw numerous people dancing around it, one of whom was his sister. He called to her and she went outside to talk, gathering her two children to her as she went. She was happy to see him, and they talked for a long time, but she didn't invite him back inside and she would not agree to come back home. This was her home now.

The brother left but he returned several times, and each time the girl would meet with him only outside. Four years passed and he never saw Judaculla for himself. One day the brother insisted on seeing the giant. His sister invited him back into the meeting chamber. She called out to her husband. A booming voice was heard from one of the darkened tunnels.

"Very well. Go back and tell all of Kanuga that they may see me. But they must first come to this meeting hall and fast for seven days. They must not leave the room or raise a war cry. After seven days, I will clothe them in new clothes and then they may see me."

The brother went back to Kanuga. The village was eager to see the giant, so they agreed to Judaculla's terms. They all journeyed to Tanasee Bald; however, among them was one man who was not from Kanuga. While the other people stayed in the hall and fasted, he would sneak outside at night and eat in secret.

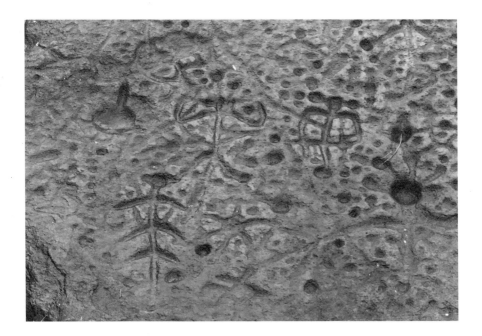

On the morning of the seventh day, a tremendous commotion was heard, like the entire side of the mountain outside was caving in. The villagers huddled together in fear. The pandemonium continued throughout the day, rising in intensity to an unbearable roar. Finally, the man who was not from Kanuga could not stand it any longer. He ran in terror from the cavern, screaming a war cry. The tumult immediately stopped. The only sound that could be heard was the stranger's screams as they faded down the mountain side.

As the seventh day ended, and it became clear that Judaculla wasn't going to show up, the villagers returned to Kanuga. But the brother stayed behind. He yelled into the darkness of the cavern, demanding to know why Judaculla didn't keep his promise. The villagers did as they were told. They did not disobey him; the stranger did. When the reply came, the voice was so loud and deep that it caused the room itself to vibrate.

"Now you will never see me."

The brother left the mountain and never returned.

In yet another legend, it is said that Judaculla Rock was created when Judaculla the giant came to North Carolina. This story says that Judaculla once lived in South Carolina, and when he decided to move north he simply made one giant leap and landed on Judaculla, creating the markings there.

And here I'll say that there is one interesting sidenote to the Judaculla story. Judaculla fits the description of the Nephilim of the Bible virtually to a tee. In Genesis, chapter 6, the Nephilim are said to be the offspring created when the lesser gods raped human women. Now I get that, depending on your point of view, that statement is either contemplative, controversial, or contradictory, but I'll just leave you to make your own conclusions and move on to the inevitable, out-of-this-world theory.

Ufologists point to the Judaculla story as proof that aliens visited Earth in the distant past. A seven-fingered giant *must* be an alien. They surmise that the marks on the rock may not be a language at all, but a star map left for future alien visitors. Proponents of this theory refer to the long connecting lines as power lines and believe they show the aliens' path through the galaxy . . . or an intergalactic trade route.

Either way, the area is well known as a UFO and paranormal hotspot. Strange lights and unidentified objects have been seen hovering over the field. Some people have even reported seeing ghosts near the rock. Of course, these claims could have a more traditional origin. For one thing, there is a graveyard just a couple hundred feet away from the field. And second, most of these reports have been made by Western Carolina University students who sneak onto the property at night. There may be a trace of alcoholic embellishment to the tales.

Now.

Do I think Judaculla or Judaculla's worm baby carved the rock? Do I think Judaculla may have been a Nephilim or one of their descendants? Or do I think the aliens left a road map on the side of Balsam Mountain?

No. No. And no.

So who DID carve Judaculla Rock? Well, I don't know! No one does.

DAN'S STORY

Our research team had the opportunity to visit Judaculla Rock on a rainy winter day, and fortunately we had the place all to ourselves. Upon arriving, we made sure to read the markers and signs that explain that Judaculla Rock is one of the country's most historically significant places, with a rich cultural legacy. It's an important ancestral landmark for the Cherokee people, but, mysteriously, there's still a lot of debate exactly as to why that's so or what it even means. It's been the subject of much study over the decades, and we're still left with what we can surmise from scholars and Indian historians.

Prior to making the trip, I spoke with numerous people who eventually got me some contact information for the property owner. I was never able to get in touch with him, but if I had, there's only one real question I'd like to ask him: What does *he* think Judaculla Rock is? I know he's heard from the experts and is undoubtedly intimately familiar with the markings, since he's seen them up close his whole life. Living in such proximity to it and having it play such a pivotal role in your life must shape your thinking and your relationship to it—it has to. Coming from that unique perspective, I'd just like to know what his heart tells him the petroglyph is trying to say.

I think perhaps we're not meant to know what it means. To be honest, I don't think the Cherokee people are meant to know either. As a landmark, it predates the Cherokee's arrival to the area. The carvings—at least some of them—were likely made long before they inhabited the land. Much like many natural occurrences and phenomena, the tribes have developed stories to explain it. But the truth is, no one really knows what it's trying to say—or how or why. It's one of the state's most incredible mysteries, with over 1,500 markings, some of which look suspiciously nonhuman.

As we arrived at the rock, we made our way downhill to the observation deck. We read several signs that displayed Cherokee symbols as we made our approach. Among my first impressions upon seeing it were that it's huge, but somehow not quite as large as I imagined. The many intricate markings weren't nearly as deep and pronounced as I had hoped. Signs displayed around the deck showed photographs and renderings of what the symbols looked like before they, unfortunately, eroded. The shape of the rock is somewhat different than what I anticipated, too, since it appears that some excavation has been done over the years to reveal more of the boulder from the ground.

The group of us wandered around the property and down a small footpath leading away from the rock and seemingly to nowhere. We felt compelled to develop theories and explanations. We were inspired to wonder. We stood around and talked about who could've been here before the Cherokee; the "native" Native Americans, if you will. Sammie hypothesized about early Viking explorers to the continent. The presence of bamboo nearby seemed out of place and helped fuel the conversation even more about who might've brought it to the area. After having recently seen the effigy of the Moon-Eyed People, we couldn't help but make connections between that carving and the similar soapstone of Judaculla. Jeff recalled that when the Cherokee came to the area, they claimed there were multiple races living in the region, the MEP being the most prominent. Were the MEP somehow descendants of early Scandinavian explorers? Could they have carved the boulder?

It was also remarked that the carvings on Judaculla looked suspiciously like European rune lines, although it was generally agreed upon that the markings on Judaculla looked to be a bit more random. Sammie hypothesized that perhaps after generations of being apart from their ancestors, the settlers had simply forgotten how to make the precise line drawings. Chad couldn't help but think that the markings on the boulder seemed reminiscent of ancient cave drawings of the so-called early astronauts, the Chariot of the Gods type of astronauts. Perhaps the markings are astrological. Standing in front of the rock, you almost half expect it to suddenly rise up out of the ground and float away like a flying saucer.

Our hypothesizing devolved to be a bit more mundane, since it seemed to me to almost resemble random doodling—like what you'd see on a notepad of mine when I'm bored and trying to concentrate. I'll start with a box, then a sphere, then pyramids, and before I know it, my paper will be filled up with sketches and symbols. They mean nothing but simply represented what popped into my head at that fleeting moment. Sammie remarked that perhaps the authors of the rock simply had bad penmanship, if you could compare writing with a pen to chiseling rock with . . . another rock.

The more you think about the effort put into Judaculla, the more it seems convincing that it had to be of some importance. It seems likely to be some form of communication with someone or something. Perhaps it's a recording of a historical event. If you squint your eyes and tilt your head, you might even think it somewhat resembles a map. Several long, straight lines almost give the appearance of a bird's-eye view of rivers. As we heard the nearby sounds of running water, this theory seemed more and more reasonable.

Standing on the observation deck, I felt an overwhelming urge to touch the rock. I suppose it's a human need to feel more connected with an object or a place or a person, to share experience through touch; however, I resisted. In order to touch Judaculla you'd have to trespass by jumping off the deck or over a fence. It is not that I wasn't able to do so; it's more a matter of respect. Witnessing such a thing in person does inspire a certain amount of respect and awe; respect not only for the mysterious artists, but also for the family and county who have worked so hard to preserve it. Over the years, so many people have touched it, lay on top of it, and done God knows what else. In the interest of conservation, I didn't want to contribute to the ever-growing erosion.

Speaking of erosion, we couldn't help but wonder where the other area petroglyphs had gone. Did they simply disappear? Legend has it that there were at least two other large petroglyphs, yet not quite as big as Judaculla, on the property. It seems highly unlikely they could have been removed. Most likely, the grounds have shifted over time because of such things as groundwater and natural erosion. Over the years, landscapes change form—and when you add human beings to the mix, with our constant interaction and construction, you can imagine how a transformation of the land might begin to take shape. I personally like to think that the Parker family has built houses and structures around the other petroglyphs in order to keep them privately hidden. To be fair, I have absolutely no evidence to back up that theory; it's just a pure gut thought.

Unfortunately, this was one of our shortest trips. It was cold and raining, and after we'd read all of the signs, looked at the rock from various angles, and had our group debates, it was time to get warm again. The observation deck affords you the opportunity to see the rock from an array of angles. If you're ever in the area and have the chance to see it in person, by all means, take it. I hope that you too can visit with a group of like-minded, curious friends who like to let their imaginations run wild.

Sammie reminded us that we were a group of grown men, standing in a circle in the middle of the woods, talking about mystical ideas and mysteries. Perhaps that's what Judaculla is really all about—sparking imagination and conversation, provoking wild thoughts and ideas. It wasn't lost on us that we were deep in conversation while standing on a trail that led to nowhere. It seemed oddly appropriate.

PART II

Piedmont Phantoms

CHAPTER 7

Ghost Train at Bostian Bridge

Statesville, North Carolina

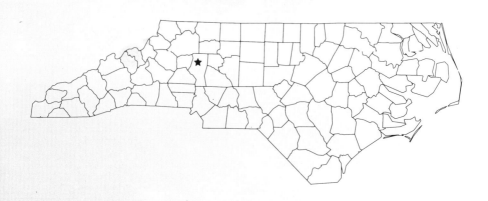

PODCAST • SEASON 3 • EPISODE 11
(January 31, 2020)

August 27, 1891

Hugh Linster arrived for work at the railway station in Statesville, North Carolina. He checked his watch: 2 a.m. He heard the familiar sound of the blow-down valve on the big steam locomotive as the engineer vented ash to ensure that the pressure pipes were clear.

He knew that the engineer and his crew had already been here for over an hour. He knew that they had performed their inspection of the locomotive and the passenger cars. He knew that the fire was being carefully stoked in the engine's hearth. He knew that the boiler had been filled to a precise level, ensuring optimal steam pressure through the system. He knew . . . well, he knew every aspect of steam train operation. And he should; he had worked here for more than forty years. He also knew that they were running behind schedule.

Finally, he heard the click-clack of the coupler as the engineer hooked up to the passenger cars. He heard the steam engine cycle as train number 9 of the Richmond and Danville Railroad Line began to pull up to the station.

He checked his watch . . . again. He knew it was 2:25 a.m., but he checked his watch anyway—his shiny new watch. He checked it because he was proud of the first new watch that he had ever owned. He checked it because he could. But mostly he checked it trying to decide if he wanted this day to hurry up and be over . . . or if he wanted it to last forever.

This was to be his last run. His last day. Hugh Linster was retiring. So he checked his shiny new watch that the R&D Railroad had given him as a retirement gift. Hugh stood on the platform with a hundred or so passengers, waiting for the train to pull up to the station. It was August, and, even at that early hour, the air was humid and sticky. But Asheville, the train's destination, would be cooler.

Finally, the train pulled up to the platform and the passengers began boarding. Hugh Linster, the baggage master, began stowing the passengers' luggage into the baggage compartment. With his task complete, Hugh looked around the platform to make sure they hadn't missed anything. The only other person on the platform was the engineer. The two men nodded to one another.

"Everything in order, Hugh?" the engineer asked.

"Yes, sir!"

As the two men boarded the train, Hugh checked his watch. It was almost 3 a.m.

But the train wouldn't make it to Asheville. It barely made it out of Statesville. On the edge of town, the tracks cut through Mrs. Bostian's property. There, Bostian Bridge crossed Third Creek. The bridge was no small feat of engineering in itself. It spanned almost 200 feet and was formed from five huge stone-and-concrete arches, the largest of which stood over 60 feet high.

The train derailed as soon as it started across the bridge, and plummeted 60 feet to the creek.

Mrs. Bostian was startled awake by the crash; in fact, the whole family was. They quickly dressed and ran out to the front porch. There, they were shocked to hear the wails of the injured. Mrs. Bostian sent her son into town to get help while she went with her grandsons to the crash site. By the time her son had come back with help, she had organized a triage of sorts. Those with the worst injuries were on her front porch, and the ones with the least serious wounds she put inside.

Two rows of dead bodies lay on the front lawn. Twenty-three people perished in the Bostian Bridge incident. Later that day, Mrs. Bostian walked slowly down the line of the deceased with a tear in her eye. No one knows what she was thinking as she did. Perhaps she asked herself the questions you ask in the wake of such a tragedy. How? Why? Or perhaps she was too stunned to think of anything at all. On she walked, looking down at their faces. Some of them she recognized. Some were unrecognizable. She stopped in front of one man. He clutched a new watch in his hand, its face as shattered as his own. Hugh Linster died that day from a broken neck.

The number 9 train had been running a bit late that fateful August morning, so the engineer had the train running full steam ahead. They hit the bridge at about 40 miles per hour. The train carried such momentum that the massive machine was airborne for 150 feet before smashing into the far bank of the creek. But, believe it or not, speed was not a factor in the accident.

The Richmond and Danville Railroad investigated the incident and found that someone had removed most of the spikes that held the tracks in place. They mounted a manhunt and detained several people, but the saboteurs wouldn't be identified for another six years, when two men were overheard bragging about selling stolen railroad spikes for scrap. Unfortunately, it was their other cellmates who overheard them. The two men were already serving a life sentence for unrelated crimes, so, really, was justice ever served for the victims of train number 9?

Exactly one year later, the Bostian family was once again startled awake by a loud crash, followed by screams and what sounded like dying moans. Fearing the worst, they all rushed to the bridge. A small rise blocked their view of the creek. As they neared the hill, a man stumbled toward them. The others rushed over the hill while Mrs. Bostian stopped to help the man. He wore a cap and his head was down, obscuring his face. He looked at the watch in his hand. Its face was smashed.

"My watch . . . ," he mumbled, obviously in shock. "Do you know the time, ma'am?"

Mrs. Bostian thought the watch seemed familiar, but she couldn't place it . . . until the man looked up at her.

"My watch . . ."

It was the face of the man who had lain dead in her yard one year ago that very day. It was Hugh Linster.

Meanwhile, the screams had faded away over the hill. She ran to the top of it and found nothing but an empty field. Her family wandered around, confused. Mrs. Bostian looked back at Hugh, but he too faded away as she watched in horror.

And so a legend was born. It was soon said that the wreck at Bostian Bridge recurs every year on the night of its anniversary. But the thing about legends is that they tend to make people *look* for something that may not be there.

For example, let's look at the story Michael Renegar tells of a man named Willie who walked home from his sister's house late one night. To get home, he would have to walk across the Bostian property. That meant he had two choices: he could either brave a barbed-wire fence, cross a pasture riddled with cow-patty land mines, cross the creek, scale another barbed-wire fence, and scurry up an embankment covered with briars, *or* he could simply walk across the bridge. He chose the bridge. About halfway across he realized his mistake.

Willie thought to himself. *Today's the twenty-seventh*, he remembered. AUGUST 27. He didn't own a watch, but he had left his sister well after midnight, so it had to be close to 3 a.m. As if on cue, he heard the huff and chug of a steam train coming toward him. He sprinted to cross the bridge before it got to him. He made it to the other side and dove off the tracks. Then a great rush of wind swept over him like a train speeding past, but he saw nothing. Well, not quite nothing. He saw the silhouette of a man cresting the hill and looking at his watch.

"Willie! Do you have any idea what time it is?" the man asked.

At 6 foot 4, 230 pounds, Willie wasn't scared of very much, but ghosts were ghosts. He screamed like a teenaged girl and ran all the way back home.

Now let's back up a bit to a few minutes before all this happened. An Iredell County sheriff's deputy was out on patrol when his vehicle stopped running. He coasted to a stop on the edge of the road while his car made all sorts of squealing and banging noises that cars just shouldn't make. He called it in and, as he waited on help . . . nature called. He looked around and decided his only option was to go over the hill beside the road and relieve himself.

As he topped the hill, he saw a man dive off the railroad tracks and into the bushes. The moon was behind him, so he recognized Willie right away. What was Willie doing out here jumping into the bushes at three in the morning? He didn't realize that Willie could see his silhouette only in the moonlight.

"Willie!" he called. "Do you have any idea what time it is?" Provoking Willie to scream and run away.

The two men would laugh about that night for years to come, but did Willie really hear a phantom train? Or was it the sheriff's ailing patrol car? A few years ago, a group of amateur ghost hunters did, indeed, encounter something on the bridge.

In Charlotte, a group of about a dozen people learned about the legend, and, being August 27, 2010, they decided on a whim to head to Statesville and see what would happen. There was no time to ask for permission to be on the property, and they did not take the time to do their due diligence in researching the situation. They arrived at the bridge just before 3:00 a.m. and spread out on and around it. Several minutes later they were astounded to hear the sound of a train coming toward them.

Now, if they had taken the time to ask the property owner or even consulted a train schedule online, they would have known that what they were hearing was a real Norfolk Southern freight train pulled by three large locomotives and barreling straight toward them. When they realized that they were in trouble, they sprinted back along the narrow bridge, but it was too late. All but two made it.

One woman jumped off the side and fell about 12 feet to the ground. She had to be rushed to a trauma center in Charlotte to treat her injuries. But twenty-nine-year-old Christopher Kaiser was struck by the train and killed.

DAN'S STORY

In late January 2020, Jeffrey Cochran and I, along with our coconspirators, Sammie Cassell and Chad Hunt, visited the Bostian Bridge, outside Statesville. Oddly enough, it's not very difficult to find, since it sits in proximity to, wait for it . . . Bostian Bridge Road. By researching properties and obsessively scanning Google maps, I predetermined a proper parking location and point of entry. As you might imagine, upon arriving at the location just as it began to sleet and snow, I was a bit relieved to find that not only was I correct in my plans, but we had easy access to the bridge itself.

Shortly after parking on a small gravel lot on the side of the road, we met with an older lady who asked if either of us were Jimmy. She wanted to let him know that one of his bulls was on her property. Once she determined we were not responsible for the steers, she quickly left in search of Jimmy. We then set off on foot, through an open gate and into a pasture that leads directly to the infamous Bostian Bridge.

My first impression of the bridge was that it's massive and still in sound structural shape. This is particularly a feat of engineering, considering the time frame in which it was erected, and in rural North Carolina. We weren't able to walk the train tracks or get close enough to touch it, because we respected the boundary of the fence in place between the pasture and the bridge, but we were left with a perfect vantage point to see not only the structure but the creek below.

My second impression was that Third Creek, which flowed under the bridge, was so full and moved with such a pace that it seemed more like a river. It seemed too deep to be considered a creek, but perhaps too shallow to be a river. But as the legend describes, you could easily see someone drowning in it. Along the posts of the bridge, which reach the ground, you can see signs of erosion near the bottom. It's obvious this is a very worn and well-traversed bridge. Jeff noticed that there was significant structural damage around the tops of the arches at multiple points along the bridge. What wasn't clear was whether or not this damage occurred as a result of the 130-year-old train crash or just due to normal wear and tear.

All over the south side of the bridge, where we had our vantage point, we observed numerous marks of graffiti. Most of these were crappy pieces of art with a few tags here and there, in easy-to-reach places. I even spotted an anarchists' "A" and some beer cans for good measure. One of the things that stood out to us as we admired the structure was the steepness of the embankment along its sides. From a cursory visual estimation, they appeared to be at about 45-degree angles. Standing next to the bridge, it was easy to see how someone might fall off the side and incur severe injury, as was the case in 2010. It was also easy to see how, even running at full speed, it would be difficult to outrun a train on such a long bridge. From one end to the other, it was a pretty damn good haul, even while running for your life.

Just as we stood by, looking around the property, I remarked to the group, "I wish we had someone from the Bostian family who could talk to us." And wouldn't you know it, we saw Jimmy riding his tractor, more than 100 yards in the distance, headed in our direction. We prepared ourselves to be told off and even cursed out by an angry property owner. Being responsible writers, and just plain people of integrity, we made a point to walk toward him and introduce ourselves.

I can't speak for the rest of the guys, but my fears were put at ease as I offered a friendly wave to the elderly gentleman, to which he instinctively returned. I then approached him as he sat on his tractor and turned the engine off so that we could talk. By this point, the sleet had turned into fat, fluffy snowflakes that were dropping at a speedy rate. I extended my hand and told him my name and advised that we were researching the bridge for this book. He almost seemed relieved that we weren't bigger troublemakers—he even remarked that he thought perhaps we were with Norfolk Southern, the railroad company that maintains the line.

Jimmy told us his full name was James Bostian Troutman, placing emphasis on his middle name, and that he was seventy-eight years old. Mr. Troutman told us that the house that belonged to his ancestors, which played a key figure in the legend, burned down in 1954. According to Jimmy, on November 22, 1963, the fateful day that President Kennedy was assassinated in Dallas, he had been walking along the creek bed underneath the bridge and located a long piece of railing that was imbedded in the ground. Jimmy said that it took a bulldozer to eventually unearth the ironwork, which turned out to be approximately 30 feet long.

He was able to confirm for us that the train fell to its resting place on the other side of the bridge from where we were standing, along the north side of the tracks. Jimmy was not very pleased about the works of graffiti that had marked the bridge, only recently by his estimation. He told us he had been in contact with the railroad company and with the local sheriff's office about reporting the vandalism. Jimmy also recalled that a nearby neighbor claimed to have spoken with a railroad detective who knocked on their door and asked that they try to keep people from trespassing on the tracks. I'm sure the concern was an attempt at curtailing a repeat of the 2010 incident.

We were all very pleased to have met Jimmy Troutman, and all remarked about what a pleasure he was to speak with. He had every right to be rude and unpleasant to us, since we encroached upon his property without prior consent; however, we found him to be very accommodating, and he seemed to tell us as much as he knew about the story and his familial connection. I'd like to take this opportunity to formally thank him for his hospitality and recognize his contribution to this telling.

On the way off the property, we met again briefly with the neighbor who was concerned about the loose cattle. She said that she had never seen anything she would call a ghost at this location, but that she had family members who have heard the crash on the anniversary of the tragic accident. She actually suggested that we come back to the location on the 27th of August in the hopes of hearing the horrific sounds repeating once again. We just might do that.

As we drove away from the scene, and as it snowed harder and harder, our group pondered the concept of anniversary ghost stories. It seems so implausible that apparitions would choose to reappear on the anniversary of their own tragic demise, just to reexperience the event. Jeff admitted that it was hard to believe because he couldn't wrap his head around the "why." We all acknowledged that it was a common enough trope in the folklore of many ghost tales. Although we don't understand it, it's hard to ignore this common thread of returning on the day of one's death, perhaps as a form of remembrance or warning. Maybe one's *death day* is the inverse of their birthday, and in turn, an apt greeting might be "Many unhappy returns."

CHAPTER 8

Lydia, the Hitchhiking Ghost

Jamestown, North Carolina

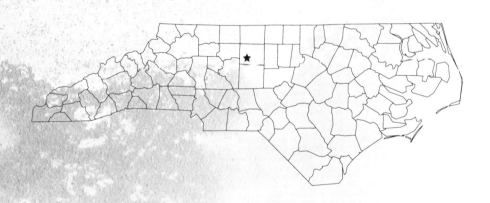

PODCAST • SEASON 1 • EPISODE 3
(October 20, 2017)

She is known by many names: the Phantom Hitchhiker, the Vanishing Lady, the Lady in White, the Lovely Apparition, the Vanishing Hitchhiker. She is probably the most well-known apparition in the state of North Carolina. She is, of course, Lydia, and she is thought to have died in Jamestown almost a hundred years ago.

On a foggy night in the spring of 1923, a beautiful young woman named Lydia was at a dance. She lost track of time before suddenly realizing she was in jeopardy of missing her curfew. She had promised her mother that she would not be too late. She found her date and they hurriedly left. The details of the conversation inside the car will never be known. Maybe they were preoccupied with talk of plans for the future. Perhaps the man, determined to have the girl home before her curfew, was simply driving way too fast for the poor road conditions. It had been raining, you see, and the thick fog made it difficult to see the curves on the narrow, twisting road. Regardless of the cause, the result is the same: the man lost control of their vehicle and they slammed into the side of the Southern Railroad Underpass Bridge.

You have to remember that cars of that era didn't offer very much in the way of safety and protection. The choice of vehicle was limited for the common man, cars such as the Ford Model T and the like. The man was killed instantly, and the car landed off the roadway. Lydia managed to crawl out of the twisted wreckage and back to the road, but no one would stop to help her. They must have mistaken her for a random hitchhiker. She died next to the mouth of the bridge.

The incident prompted the saddened and outraged town of Jamestown into building a new railroad bridge and straightening out some of the blind curves on the dangerous section of road.

A few years later, a man named Burke Hardison (not his real name) was visiting friends in Raleigh. On his way home to High Point, he too encounters a woman in a white dress, standing under the bridge in Jamestown. People were far less suspicious back then, so he pulls over to offer her a ride. She gets in the car without answering, and Burke notices that the girl's dress is torn and dirty. The man asks her if she's hurt, but all she says is that she needs to get home before her mother starts to worry. He tries to drum up conversation with the girl, but all he gets is the same answer. The girl points out a house, and the man pulls over to the curb. He gets out, runs around the car, and opens the door for her—but no one is there.

The man is confused but also intrigued. There was no way the girl could have gotten out of the car without him noticing, but . . . where else could she have gone? Despite the late hour, he wants to make sure the girl made it inside safely. He braves the storm and walks up to knock on the door of the house. An elderly woman answers and is not entirely surprised to see him. He explains what had happened and asks if the girl is okay.

The old woman sadly shakes her head and tells him that the girl was her daughter Lydia, who passed away in a car accident thirty years ago. She says that he's not the first person who has tried to get her daughter home to her.

Since then there have been a dozen different variations of the story, but essentially it is always the same. For example, some versions of the story say that every year on the anniversary of her death, someone attempts to bring Lydia home to her mother. Other tellings say that she appears only on dark and stormy nights. Sometimes she had been attending a New Year's Eve ball; sometimes it's the high school prom. Sometimes the dress is covered in blood. Some stories say that they collided with another car head-on and that both Lydia and her date were killed instantly.

Almost as numerous as the differing accounts of Lydia's story is the address where she asks to be taken. Although most versions of the stories never say the address, those that do have said that it was on Johnson Street. Other reports put it on Woodleaf, or Maple, or Walnut, or even Centennial— which was how I heard it growing up. Some of those streets no longer exist, but street names tend to change.

The village of Jamestown, North Carolina, was first settled in the 1770s and was established in 1816 by George Mendenhall as a Quaker village. High Point Road, the road where Lydia's ghost is seen, was one of the first wagon trails through the area and remained nothing more than a packed-dirt path for nearly a hundred years. In 1908, it was resurfaced as a macadam road, a method of road construction that involved pressing crushed rock to form a gravel road. These gravel roads presented a couple of problems, one of which was dust. This issue was alleviated with the invention of tarmac. Contrary to modern colloquialism, tarmac does not mean asphalt for an airport runway; tarmac was an earlier version of asphalt that was a mixture of coal tar and ironworks slag. What we know as asphalt today was not used until the mid-1920s.

You may be asking, What's the point? The point is, the road that Lydia and her date traveled in 1923 was not the well-maintained blacktop that we're accustomed to today in "the Good Roads State." A fact that, coupled with their high speed, probably contributed to the accident that caused the couple's untimely death.

The Path of High Point Road (US 29-70A) has been altered since that fateful night; the original underpass is about 100 feet west of the new one. During the warm months, it is barely visible at all through the kudzu that grows there. Yet, none of that has stopped the sightings of Lydia. She seems to have found her way to the new bridge.

In 1966, Frank Fay was driving High Point Road late one night. He and his wife were taking another couple home to High Point from Greensboro. When they neared the infamous bridge, they saw a girl in white attempting to flag down the car in front of them. Even though the car in front of them did not stop, the girl tried to open the door as it passed by. Mr. Fay slowed, but when he got to the bridge, the girl was nowhere to be seen. He was sure that she had not gotten in the car ahead of them, since it had never even touched its brakes. It was as if the driver hadn't seen the girl at all.

When Frank asked if anyone else had seen what he had, they had all seen the same thing.

Tom Beasley and Rick Cook, however, had a very different experience in 1976. It was late, 1 or 2 a.m., and they were headed toward High Point. It was, once again, a rainy, miserable night. As Tom crested the hill that leads down to the underpass, he saw a girl in a white dress standing on the side of the road. He asked Rick if he had seen the same thing, but Rick looked at him like he was crazy. Rick hadn't seen anything. Frustrated, Tom turned the car around, and this time both men saw the girl. They turned around once more; by now the girl was sitting down in the gravel beside the road. Tom stopped the car and Rick rolled his window down. Rick leaned out to ask if the girl needed a ride, but no words came out of her mouth. "Drive," Rick said to Tom quietly as he leaned back inside the car.

Tom sighed and urged his friend to ask if the girl was okay. "Just get us out of here," Rick said, rolling up the window. There was something about the tone of Rick's voice that frightened Tom, prompting him to do as he was told. As Tom stomped on the gas pedal, he could hear the girl yelling for him to come back. Tom, of course, asked Rick what the hell was going on. Rick said that there was something wrong with the girl. She was covered in blood and looked as if someone had beaten her. They were afraid to go back and check.

Did Tom and Rick see the ghost of Lydia or was it just a high school prank? They didn't realize that they may have seen Lydia's ghost until they told the story to some friends a few days later. They felt guilty about not going back, but something about the whole thing gave them the creeps. There hadn't been any reports of an injured girl on the news, and the more they talked about it, the stranger the night seemed.

Tom says that he still thinks about going back out there today to see if he can find her again. He's still shaken up by the experience but says that if he saw her again, he would help her. This time he would *make* her get it the car, ghost or not.

Of course, a story this well known will have its fair share of practical jokesters. Many people, mostly high school students, have staged various hoaxes, ranging from very simple to quite elaborate. Some have convinced a female student to walk up and down the road wearing a white dress. Another group was caught dangling a dress from strings over the road.

Lydia isn't alone.

Jamestown isn't the only place out there to have a phantom hitchhiker story. Stories of phantom hitchhikers have been around for hundreds of years. The ancient Romans had a similar tale more than 1,000 years ago. A hitchhiking ghost appears in a 1602 book about ghost stories. The vanishing hitchhiker tale has made dozens of appearances in dozens of cities. In fact, there is a comparable story to be found in almost every major city. Every state in the union boasts at least one vanishing hitchhiker, including FOUR others in North Carolina. Many point to the fact that there *are* so many as possible proof that this type of residual presence is feasible.

Most of these stories are dismissed as urban legend, but Lydia's story is different. It is perhaps the most detailed story of all phantom hitchhiker stories, with a very defined backstory. Even if the story of Lydia is not completely true, perhaps it's somewhat based on actual events. Did she really exist?

Whether she is real or not, Lydia will always hold a special place in the hearts of those who believe and those who love North Carolina ghost stories. As long as storytelling exists, so will Lydia, whether she be legend or tragedy; the premature death of a beautiful woman is made all the more tragic by the fact that no matter how hard she tries, she can never go home.

One controversial theory behind Lydia's origin has been presented by a psychic who claims that Lydia could be a thought form, having neither lived nor died. A tulpa is a term originating from the Tibetan word for "manifestation." It is believed, in certain circles, that if enough people believe something is true, they can unknowingly cause it to exist. The new being, the thought form, will carry out the actions that those who created it expect it to carry out. Thus, someone who has never been to Jamestown or never heard of Lydia may see a girl in need of a ride, pick her up, and *try* to take her home.

As far-fetched as this seems, there is also the "Phillip experiment." Supposedly a group of psychics got together and made up a fictitious person. They named him Phillip. They also wrote a fake background story for the person. Then, through various mediums, they were able to contact the spirit of Phillip, who told them details that they had written down in his backstory.

Okay, I'll be the first to say that there's a whole lot of unexplained things out there in the world, but . . . really? I don't know how much stock I give to "a ghost exists because we think it exists." If that were true, I'd imagine we'd be seeing them everywhere we turned.

Lydia is such a huge part of North Carolina ghost lore. Many people would be deeply saddened to find out that she never existed. Of course, we each believe what we believe—meaning that some people will believe that she exists, no matter what kind of evidence is found to the contrary, and others will always say that she has never been real, no matter what. And that's fine: but I would advocate doing so after educating yourself and not taking *everything* at face value.

Several people are convinced that Lydia was a real person and have attempted the arduous task of looking for her true identity. In fact, some people have been downright obsessed with it. Why does it matter if she was a real person or not? These researchers seem to think that if they can find the person who inspired these stories that it will add veracity to the claims. For those who have witnessed the apparition, I'm sure they don't need to know the girl's name to make it any more real for them.

One researcher undertook an extensive search of newspaper accounts and death records of the early 1920s to try to definitively identify who Lydia may be. She found no death certificates for a Lydia in Guilford County for that time frame. Likewise, when the author scoured decades of newspaper articles, she did not find a match to the described accident.

Another reporter searched police records for a field report of an accident in 1923. He tried Jamestown and High Point to no avail. Next, he tried the Guilford County Sheriff's Department, and still he found no record of the accident. That, however, doesn't really prove anything; after more than ninety years, records can be misplaced or accidentally destroyed. He also tried the State Highway Patrol, but they weren't even established until 1929. He tried the Department of Motor Vehicles, but they keep records for only ten years. He, too, had hit a dead end.

One woman *claims* to have investigated the mystery at the Guilford County Register of Deeds, which is responsible for keeping death certificates of anyone who died in that county. She says that she has found five Lydias who died in 1923. Four were quickly dismissed as not *the* Lydia because the records showed that they did not die in a car accident. She claims to have found a fifth girl, Lydie Underwood, whose death records were missing. It seems too good to be true. This reporter was searching the death records and found a name, but not a record? So where did the name come from? Why has no one else been able to duplicate this finding?

So what does that all mean? Does it mean that she's not real? Not necessarily. The witnesses seem pretty adamant that they saw what they saw. Does it mean that she was, indeed, Lydie Underwood? It's possible, but I don't think so. Perhaps Lydia wasn't her real name, but a nickname. Perhaps she and her mother were visiting Guilford County and did not live there. In short, it proves absolutely nothing. And for me, that's okay; sometimes we don't need to know.

And who says she died in 1923, anyway? That year was adopted from Burke Hardison's story when the mother told him that her daughter had died "last year." She also said that he wasn't the first to try to bring her home, and that every year someone makes the same attempt. Both statements indicate that the year of Lydia's death may have been several years earlier than 1923. Who knows?

Some claim that the year is correct but that her name is not. Burke Hardison admitted that when the girl spoke, it was so low that he could barely hear her. One author claims to have spoken directly to several elderly people during the '80s and '90s while doing research for a book he was writing. There have been numerous fatal accidents on that stretch of road throughout the years, but he found a few people who remembered one from the approximate time frame. Two of them said it had happened in 1923, but the others all gave different years, going as far back as 1911. The only thing that they all agreed on . . . Lydia was *not* the girl's name. Those who could recall a name said that it had been Mary, or Mary Anne, or Marion, or something to that effect.

And now, it seems, there is new evidence to support this theory. Michael Renegar is one of those people who have been obsessed by the Lydia myth over the years. He recently released his third book about Lydia, along with Amy Greer, titled *Looking for "Lydia": The Thirty-Year Search for the Jamestown Hitchhiker*. In it, he claims to have found a *Greensboro Patriot* newspaper article detailing the death of Annie Jackson. On June 21, 1920, both Annie and Dorothy Beck were killed when the vehicle they were operating overturned in the vicinity of the infamous Jamestown Underpass. Renegar is convinced that Lydia was actually Annie L. Jackson. And to be honest, he makes a pretty good argument. Perhaps the century-old mystery has been solved after all. Check his book out and see for yourself.

DAN'S STORY

Few ghost stories are tied to a specific location the way Lydia is to the small suburb of Jamestown. Nestled right between the cities of Greensboro and High Point, in the southwestern region of Guilford County, Jamestown is famously known for this tale. The town isn't shying away from it either; as a matter of fact, it's leaning into it. As of the time of this writing, the town council has just recently broken ground on the brand-new walkway that's designed to connect people to the infamous overpass where Lydia was said to have died. The bridge has become known as "Lydia's Bridge" and can be seen approximately 50 feet southwest of the roadway where the current bridge now stands.

I moved to Greensboro in the summer of 2007 to attend graduate school. Being a lifelong admirer of local ghost stories and folklore, I was familiar with the tale, but not intimately. I began learning about the hitchhiking ghost through local newspaper articles and various websites. Eventually, I sought out and attended a live reading of the story by Cynthia Moore Brown at a historic cemetery in the heart of Greensboro. She's an amazing oral storyteller (much better than I) and helps keep alive the tradition passed down by our elders. Her rendition of Lydia's story is especially good. While its tone and dramatic style are mostly geared toward a younger audience, it'll entertain even the most cynical adult.

It wasn't until I was beginning the original iteration of *Carolina Haints* in 2010 that I actually visited Lydia's bridge for myself. My wife, Lauren, and I decided to make the short trip to Jamestown, just a few minutes from our old house. The descriptions found online were spot on; the ominous opening of the underpass was nestled in the side of the hill. At this point in time, the brush surrounding the opening was fairly maintained—which would not always be the case. We parked our car in a nearby apartment complex parking lot and made our way through the grass.

Upon our approach, we found the bridge to be littered with random acts of graffiti, much like its modern counterpart a few feet away. But there were also plenty of signs that indicated others had come to this spot, and with much regularity. Among the creepiest things we found was fresh-looking red paint, written in a crazy style on the side of the wall reading "Lydia . . ."

We also found a makeshift spirit board lying on the ground. It appeared to have been hastily put together on the back of a piece of cardboard. I don't recall seeing a planchet nearby, but there was writing on the board itself that stated, "Lydia, go toward the light, not that light, the other light at the end of the tunnel."

We made our recording and were honestly just tickled to be there. Of course, we didn't see anything supernatural or frightening. After all, we made our initial visit in the middle of the afternoon on a bright, sunny day; however, the next time we encountered a cold, rainy night, I made sure to revisit. I've since come through

that same stretch of road hundreds of times, even on cold, rainy nights. I've never seen anything that resembles a hitchhiking ghost in a white gown, but that doesn't stop me from looking.

One time I visited the infamous bridge while geocaching. I'm not much of a geocacher anymore, but for a while there, my wife and I were really into it. If you're not familiar with it, it's a pretty neat hobby. You're given GPS coordinates and must find the location of a hidden treasure. Once you've found it, you can sign the logbook and rehide it for the next geocacher. I made a trip to the bridge and found a very cool cache hidden in an ammo can, suspended from a tree. I located the line, attached to a spike in the ground, and followed it to a tree branch where it was wrapped up, then continued to follow it until I found the cache, camouflaged so it wouldn't be noticeable to passersby. This particular cache was a special one because I was able to combine it with my love for horror movies and take a DVD while leaving one in return. If my memory serves me, I left a DVD of *The Amityville Horror* (1979).

While I was at that location, approximately 30 feet deep in the woods from Lydia's bridge, I decided to go check out the bridge itself and see what was new. Every time I've visited the site, I've seen new and interesting artwork on the walls. On this occasion, I came across a somewhat disturbing find. Along the north corner of the outside wall, I found what appeared to be a pipe bomb. My first reaction was to freeze and back up, which I'm sure was exactly what the bomb maker wanted; however, curiosity got the better of me and I decided to check it out a little closer for myself before calling 911.

Upon closer inspection, it seemed pretty apparent that the bomb was in fact not a bomb at all, but a toy designed to look like a bomb and undoubtedly give whoever found it a good scare. I must say, it worked. The irony of the situation was not lost on me—the story of a guy interested in ghost stories being taken out by a bomb at the sight of a famous ghost story. Don't get me wrong—had I been blown up that day, I would've likely joined Lydia in her quest to scare people at that bridge.

But I lived to tell the tale, and today as I write this entry I'm very excited to visit the new walkway currently under construction. I'm proud of the leaders of Jamestown for having the idea and then seeing it through; not just to be known for a piece of folklore but to own it and encourage people to come be a part of it. As with every story of ghosts and ghouls in the Carolinas, I don't care if it's real or not—the story and the life it continues to have is what's interesting.

But enough from me. Let's hear from someone who knows firsthand about the story, because they've lived it. I was fortunate to get to speak with Tom Beasley, who, along with a friend, had a run-in with Lydia in the early '70s. While Tom himself does believe in ghosts, he'll tell you, "You know, if somebody asks me specifically about what I saw, would I 1,000 percent say that I saw a ghost? No. Because to me, it looked like a person standing on the side of the road." He went on to add, "Do I believe in ghosts? Yes, I do. Not because of that, but yeah, I believe in them. Do I think they have to be a spirit that I can see through, and they can levitate? No, I don't believe that. So, by the same token, I'm not saying I didn't see one. I just wouldn't 1,000 percent say that I did. The only thing I can say was that it was a damn strange situation."

I asked Tom if he had kept in touch with Rick Cook, who had been his passenger that fateful night. He told me that Cook declined to participate in a documentary TV episode of the show *Monsters and Mysteries in America* in which Tom appeared, but discussed the episode with him afterward. Tom said he asked Rick, "Why wouldn't you be in the film? You at least saw something different than I did. Even if you have a whole different version of what I've told, that would be great." Tom said that Rick didn't say a word right away but eventually said something that Tom thought was a little strange: "Man, I don't know why, but that scared me so bad."

This still baffles Tom, who looks back at it and told me, "All these years later, he still thinks that. Maybe he just doesn't want to talk about it. For him to keep silent for this many years says what a strong impression it made on him. I mean, that's a long time, man! I mean forty years later, he still has that sensitivity about it." I asked him if he still drives down that stretch of road, and he said that of course he does. He didn't avoid the area after seeing Lydia but said he certainly doesn't go out there looking for her.

I asked Tom what he thought of the various accounts of his story found in print and in the TV show. Tom said, "A lot of people try to tell the story, and they've got a story to write and are trying to sell books. I do not blame them any bit at all as to whatever they wrote; they had a book to write. And does it matter to me personally? No, I don't care what they wrote. Of all the things that have been written, I think Michael Renegar's *Looking for Lydia* is probably the closest as anything could come. And the show, in my opinion, was really close to it too." But he takes objection with the way Lydia is portrayed when she appears to hiss with vampire fangs.

Tom refers to Michael Renegar as *the authority* on the subject of Lydia, and rightfully so. Michael believes he's discovered the true identity of Lydia in Annie Luda Jackson and makes a damn strong case for it in his book. At the point of rewriting this entry, I couldn't help but notice how close we're getting to June 20, 2020, the centennial anniversary of Annie Jackson's untimely death. As we've discussed in other chapters of this book, the anniversary element of ghost stories seems to be a recurring theme. Perhaps yours truly will find himself at Lydia's bridge on that date. Stay tuned, dear readers . . .

CHAPTER 9

The Legend of Peter Dromgoole

Chapel Hill, North Carolina

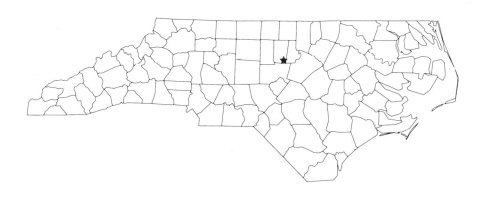

PODCAST • SEASON 2 • EPISODE 1
(September 21, 2018)

The story of Peter Dromgoole is a thing of legend. Legend in its truest sense: a story, at least in part, based in truth but perverted by the passage of time and contorted by the embellishment of retelling until, at last, the story as we know it may have very little truth remaining. So what is the story of Peter Dromgoole? It begins, as many of these legends do, as a love story.

Peter came to Chapel Hill in 1833 and fell in love with a girl named Fannie. Day after day the two lovers would meet by a rather large rock near the campus of the University of North Carolina, at a place called Piney Prospect, or Piney Point.

But before Peter Dromgoole came to Chapel Hill, Fannie had another suitor—one whom she had rejected in favor of Peter. One evening Peter crossed paths with the jilted suitor on campus. Angry words were exchanged, and before long the two had agreed to meet the following morning for a duel. The university considered its students and faculty to be men of the utmost character, so dueling was strongly discouraged in the student handbook.

The morning's dawn rose on the two gentlemen as they prepared for battle; ironically, at the very rock where Peter and Fannie usually met. Word of the duel had spread among the students, and a small crowd had gathered to witness the events.

Now, I'd like to tell you that Peter fought him off . . . but he didn't. His rival shot him clean through the heart, and Peter collapsed on the fateful rock at Piney Point. Part of the legend claims that the rock has forever been stained red by the flow of Peter's blood.

At this point the gravity of the situation began to settle upon the bystanders. The shooter and several of those in attendance quickly buried Peter's body under the rock and swore to never speak of it again. But, of course, there had been too many witnesses, and to imagine that a group of university students could ever keep such a thing a secret was folly.

Fannie had no knowledge of the duel and came to Piney Point that afternoon as always. Of course, Peter was not there . . . at least not that she could see. She left heartbroken but returned day after day, waiting for her lover to come back to her.

Soon the rumors began to churn, and, in a desperate attempt to take the spotlight off himself, the shooter claimed that Peter had run off to join the army. Talk of murder persisted, however, and Peter's rival was forced to abandon his studies and leave town.

Eventually, Fannie stopped coming to the rock, but her broken heart never mended. A year later, on the anniversary of Peter's death, Fannie succumbed to her grief and also passed away. The blood-stained rock has become known as Dromgoole Rock, and, from time to time, people claim to see the ghostly apparition of two young lovers around the area.

As with most legends, through retelling and retelling, many variations of the story have been presented. In some versions, Fannie hears about the duel and shows up just in time to see Peter slump against their rock. She runs to him and he dies in her arms.

Some tell that the duel was with pistols following a dance at the university; others say it was with swords and took place between Peter and a professor after an argument in class. Some have it at dawn, others at noon, while other versions say it happened at midnight. Occasionally, the tale is told with the unnamed rival being Peter's best friend.

It's even been said that Peter was victorious in the duel, but that then he panicked and rode off into the sunset . . . never to be seen again.

Also, in keeping with the tradition of most legends, there are naysayers who say that none of the above events ever took place.

Now, the first question in any good legend is "Did this person even exist?" The answer appears to be . . . yes!

As for Fannie and the unnamed duelist, neither their full names nor their true part of Peter's story has ever definitively been proven; however, the Dromgoole family was well known throughout the worlds of both politics and religion through Virginia and the Carolinas. Peter's grandfather was Reverend Edward Dromgoole, an Irish immigrant who was fundamental in the spread of the Methodist religion in the region. His father, Edward Dromgoole II, was not only another renowned minister, but also a merchant, planter, and physician. Peter's uncle was a respected Virginia congressman.

Peter grew up in the Roanoke Rapids area of Virginia with his younger brother, Edward Dromgoole III. Peter's father wished for him to attend the University of North Carolina, and in 1833 Peter arrived in Chapel Hill. He applied for acceptance to UNC but was rejected—in those days the admittance exam was heavily steeped in Greek and Latin. But Peter did not return home. He acquired a tutor and told his father that he would easily pass the admittance test next year. His father was very disappointed but reluctantly allowed Peter to stay in Chapel Hill.

I suppose it is at this point you must decide for yourself which path Peter took with his life. Did he fall in love with Fannie only to be murdered by a rival? Or, as many believe, did he succumb to the many temptations that beset every freshman when they find themselves on their own for the first time in their lives? There exists a letter dated April 1833 from William Hooper, a Chapel Hill professor, addressed to Peter's father. In it, the professor reports that Peter had fallen into many bad habits: drinking, womanizing, card playing, and horse racing. Professor Hooper claims that Peter had become a distraction to the other students, and he implored for Edward Dromgoole to intercede.

This, of course, strikes a completely opposite image of Peter as we've come to know from the legend. Was this intervention the wake-up call that he needed to turn his life around? Or was he, in fact, simply a rich, spoiled troublemaker? Some would say the campus of UNC is still riddled with such men . . . and women.

Regardless, after receiving the letter, Edward Dromgoole did, indeed, write Peter and demand that he return home at once. This led to a series of heated letters between the two. Peter finally told his father, "I have determined never more to see that parent's face whom I have treated with so little respect."

Soon after this, Peter disappeared, leaving behind all of his possessions, and was never seen or heard from again. There are several theories as to where he may have gone, assuming of course that he isn't buried under Dromgoole Rock. He had claimed that he was going to run away to Europe, and many believe that he did just that.

The university sent his books and possessions to his father when his room was found empty. His father believed that he left school and went west, where he was robbed and murdered. A popular theory is that he changed his name to John Williams and enlisted in the army at Smithville (known today as Southport).

There was, in fact, a John Williams who joined the army in 1834 and thrived under the military discipline. He rose quickly through the ranks but was shot and killed while on guard duty during the Second Seminole War in 1835. John Williams is buried in the St. Augustine National Cemetery. There is no real proof that John Williams was really Peter Dromgoole, unless you count the fact that Dromgoole's roommate at Chapel Hill was named . . . wait for it . . . John Williams.

As for the infamous duel, Peter's uncle, Virginia congressman George Dromgoole, survived a duel in 1837. He killed a man named Daniel Dugger in a duel on the banks of the Roanoke River in Northampton County, North Carolina. Those who believe Peter simply ran away are convinced that his uncle's duel was mistakenly incorporated into Peter's story.

So what actually happened to Peter Dromgoole? As is the way with legends, no one knows for sure.

Dromgoole Rock sits on private property, and, to the best of my knowledge, no excavation has ever been done to see if there really was a body buried beneath it.

The mysterious red "blood" stains of Dromgoole Rock may have a scientific explanation rather than a supernatural one. If you search the area, you'll find that many of the rocks there have reddish discoloration. Geologists credit this to rust from the high iron content of the rock's composition.

For fifty years Peter's story remained campus folklore. It wasn't until the late 1800s that it saw a resurgence in popularity. At that point, the tale began to appear in novels and magazine articles. Over the following century, it's retold and reimagined in dozens of novels, short stories, and documentaries.

Around the same time, UNC's version of the Skull and Bones Society was formed. Perhaps it was not a coincidence that the Dromgoole story saw renewed popularity around the same time. Chapel Hill's secret society was born as the Order of the Dromgoole in 1889. They soon changed their name "in accord with midnight and graves and weirdness," the founders claimed, from Dromgoole to Gimghoul.

It isn't unusual for a secret society to mask their activities by using a popular legend, so Peter's story was perfect. Their full name is now the Knights of the Order of Gimghouls, which has its foundations in Arthurian legend and the Knights of the Round Table. The original founder, Edward Wray Martin, was obsessed with medieval legend and organized the structure of the order based on chivalry, courage, loyalty, and truth.

In the 1920s, the order bought Piney Prospect, the location of Peter's demise, and began construction on a meeting place worthy of their self-envisioned prestigious status. It's claimed that French stonemasons were employed to fashion Hippol Castle from 1,300 tons of rock. The edifice was later renamed Gimghoul Castle and is listed in the International Registry of Castles. It's the cornerstone of the Gimghoul Neighborhood Historic District, an affluent section of Chapel Hill. Very little is known of the inner doings of

the order (otherwise it wouldn't be a secret society) other than that they extend invitations only to influential male junior and senior students and faculty. A list of current members is impossible to find, but some of the past members include names that are still seen around the UNC campus: Wilson, Kenan, Carmichael, Ehringhaus, Mangum, Ruffin, Craige.

There is one unsettling thing that the order cannot deny. In contrast to the order's basis in chivalry and loyalty is its motif and symbolism: the devil. The image of Satan appears in the order's original emblem. Only a handful of photographs are known to have been taken inside the castle, but imagery of the devil can be seen in nearly every one of them.

What is the meaning of the symbol's recurrence to an order dedicated to the principles of knighthood? It's obvious that the order has had prominent campus figures and successful North Carolinians among its membership. It's been surmised that the devil motif is to remind themselves that no matter how successful they become, they are still only human.

DAN'S STORY

One of the blessings and curses of writing this book is remembering trips I've made to some of these locations. It's a blessing because I'm a nostalgic person by nature. I love to reminisce over old photos of my kids. Hell, somewhere I still have a box of old love letters my wife wrote me twenty years ago when we were high school kids. So, in that sense, it's nice to look back and hear how young my voice sounded ten years ago. But as a filmmaker, the curse is having to cringe at the horrible quality of material I was putting out there into the world.

I visited Gimghoul Castle, near campus, in the Gimghoul Historic District, a decade prior to writing this entry. My wife, Lauren, and I were accompanied by my friend Michelle as we made our way down Gimghoul Road to the dead end where it turns into a gravel driveway. Being ever mindful about trespassing on private property, we parked our vehicle in the driveway and walked to the front door. I rang the doorbell, but no one came to the door.

We then walked around the perimeter of the small stone castle in search of someone to speak with. There was a large fire pit area, where it's easy to imagine a group of the order's members in cloaks standing around a roaring fire. There's a large rock in the backyard that we assumed might be the famous Peter Dromgoole rock at Piney Prospect, but we couldn't confirm the sight of blood or a rust-colored stain. The only thing we really found were some empty plastic trash cans around back, which I imagine were recently full of beer bottles and Solo cups.

We found a footpath leading eastbound away from the castle, and decided to take the trail. I remember taking it a good distance but never coming across anyone or anything. We never reached the end of the trail. A search on Google Maps shows that the trail runs around 1,200 feet from the castle to Greenwood

Road. Walking the trail, I pictured Peter and his lover traversing these woods, and the long, solemn walk she must have had the day he died.

It's said that the order is the guardian of a long-held secret—and as you may have imagined, I have some theories. Members of the order are said to be inducted by legacy or by invitation only. Unlike other secret fraternities, such as the Skull and Bones at Yale, its members aren't thought to necessarily be of particular influence or having a political agenda. Not unlike other fraternities, I think it's mainly a private social club, with emphasis on the private. My theory is that it's a club where like-minded young, white men can party as hard as they want, drink whatever they want, do whatever kind of drugs they want, and have sex with whomever they want.

I honestly don't think there's much more of a point to the Order of the Gimghoul than to have a private place to meet and for fellowship with a group of individuals who share a common interest of being able to party anonymously. Not that the other members don't know who they are, but to party in the safety that they'll keep secret the things they've seen and experienced, as part of their membership. I will say, however, the demonic mascot that adorns several drawings and shows up in old photographs is quite intriguing and opens a Pandora's box of questions about ties to the Illuminati or the Church of Satan, etc. It leaves my mind wondering about what nefarious plans are being made and executed on these grounds.

Perhaps the demonic symbology is a simple use of misdirection to make people think there's more going on here than a private social club. If so, it's working.

CHAPTER 10

The Devil's Tramping Ground

Harper's Crossroads, North Carolina

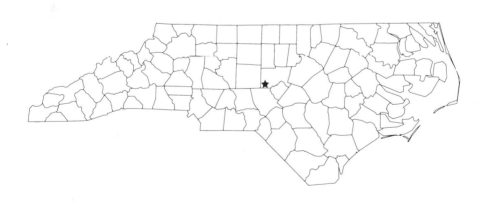

The area around Siler City, North Carolina, is mostly rural farms and wooded land . . . like most of Chatham County. But a few miles south of Siler City on State Road 1100 is a bare patch of dirt.

Yep.

That's it.

No bells. No whistles. No fireworks.

Just a bare strip of earth.

So what makes this unassuming, vegetation-free clearing any different from the millions of bare patches of dirt all around the world? That would be *legend*.

The story claims that the devil himself comes to this spot every night, pacing around and around, devising fresh evils to unleash on our world. It's this act that has given the spot its name: the Devil's Tramping Ground. Before the Moravians expanded into North Carolina, the immigrant population was predominantly from Ulster, an area bordering England and Scotland. As such, the devil was an integral part of their culture. Any strange or unexplained location would very often be named Devil's Something. North Carolina has the Seven Devils, Kill Devil Hills, Devil's Rock, Devil's Stairs, Devil's Courthouse, Devil's Branch, Devil's Chimney, Devil's Head, Devil's Knob, two different places known as the Devil's Fork, four known as the Devil's Elbow . . . and there's even a Devil's Tater Patch.

Over the past three hundred years, our expectation of the devil has changed somewhat. As movies like *The Exorcist* creep toward their fiftieth birthdays, if the devil were to materialize today, we would expect something more impressive than just walking around in a circle.

But that's the legend; the devil comes to his tramping ground at night to . . . pace.

Modern man and his science have attempted to find a rational explanation for the lack of greenery with the Devil's Tramping Ground's borders—salt, they say. The ground has a higher-than-normal salinity. This seems more like a symptom as opposed to a cause. Perhaps a better question is, Why?

Why is there just one perfectly round salt deposit in the middle of the millions of acres of woods in Chatham County? It would seem that if it were a natural feature, there would be more patches scattered throughout the area, but there simply aren't.

Not to mention the other peculiarities about the Devil's Tramping Ground that *salt* simply doesn't explain. Like why birds refuse to nest in the trees around the area. Or why dogs are reluctant to enter the circle after nightfall. Or why sticks and debris left in the tramping ground overnight will be found scattered among the surrounding trees the next morning.

Further testing by the North Carolina State Department of Agriculture determined that the soil within the circle is completely sterile. But, again, why? How?

Soil is regenerative. Any farmer can tell you that if you overplant a field, the nutrients can be leached from the soil. But by not planting in that field for a couple of years, the soil will return to normal. Most of the time all it takes is alternating between two different crops from year to year. It's called crop rotation. But it's been more than a couple of years, and the Devil's Tramping Ground still hasn't recovered. It's actually been more than two hundred years.

Now, there are also some more down-to-earth theories about the site—depending on your definition of "down to earth." Some say that it is not a place of the devil, but rather the sacred site of an ancient Native American tribe. This story tells how the tribe would gather in this area, which was known to them as the Great Flats. The tribe would feast and dance throughout the night, their moccasined feet stomping down the vegetation. This pleased the old gods so much that they blessed the tribe and the site, preserving it forever.

Another story, or rather a couple of them, is about a great battle between two rival tribes. The first version of this story says that there was so much blood spilled on this area that no vegetation is able to grow there. The other version says that King Croatoan was killed in the battle and was buried under the Devil's Tramping Ground. In both versions, the survivors of the losing Croatoan tribe fled to the coast, where they became the tribe in the Lost Colony saga.

This story may not technically be a theory behind the tramping grounds, but some years ago, a couple of men got it into their heads that there was buried treasure under the circle. So they grabbed some shovels and started digging. They dug quite a hole before they were caught, but they didn't find a treasure. Today, their hole has mostly filled in, but a slight divot still remains.

And, of course, there are the UFO conspiracists. There are some who claim the Devil's Tramping Ground is a UFO hotspot. They say that some sort of strange alien radiation that is undetectable by our primitive science has left the ground sterile.

People have also reported seeing strange lights in the area at night. But they have also reported seeing red eyes watching them from the treeline and shadowy figures moving around, just out of clear sight. A few folks said they were lulled to sleep by a beautiful, melodic voice. When they awoke, they found themselves inexplicably miles away from the tramping ground.

Now . . .

Here's something I don't get to say nearly often enough: the invisible UFO radiation theory is NOT the strangest idea associated with the Devil's Tramping Ground. There is a group that has proposed changing the name of the circle to the Chatham County Vortex. They say that the site is a "Magdalene Crystal Column of Energy."

So what the hell does that mean? I'm not entirely sure, but bear with me and I'll explain it the best I can. If there are any followers of the Magdalene Flame reading this, forgive me if I get it a little bit wrong.

It begins with the notion of male and female spiritual energies. This theory recognizes Jesus Christ as just one of the many manifestations of the male energy, along with Mohammad, Buddha, and several other spiritual leaders. By extension, Mary Magdalene, also known as the Divine Feminist, was just one representation of the female spirit.

This has evolved as a movement known as the Magdalene Flame, incorporating a Jungian mysticism, a legend that claims Jesus once visited England, and feminist retellings of Arthurian legends. They believe that a Magdalene Energy exists as a web of divine energy around the globe, touching down at various energy nodes . . . such as the Devil's Tramping Ground.

In pop culture, the Devil's Tramping Ground has appeared in two books written by Poppy Z. Brite. Both *Lost Souls* and *Drawing Blood* are set in part in North Carolina. If you haven't read it, *Lost Souls* was probably my favorite book of the 1990s. *Drawing Blood*, while not exactly a sequel, features many of the same characters.

And before any of you say that there has not been a movie made featuring the Devil's Tramping Ground . . . I scoff in your general direction! There are at least two, both aptly named *The Devil's Tramping Ground*. One was directed by Will Huneycutt and Andy Kahn in 2007. This film was written by our filmmaking friend Jaysen Buterin from Greensboro and stars Jaysen and his wife, Kindal. The second film was made in 2018 by a Nashville-based company and was directed by Weiss Night. This film is currently being shown on Amazon Prime Video.

Of course, let's not forget other forms of inspiration. The Aviator Brewing Company in nearby Fuquay-Varina makes a 9.2 percent Belgium Tripel called Devil's Tramping Ground.

The Devil's Tramping Ground is about 10 miles south of Siler City on State Road 1100, which has officially been renamed Devil's Tramping Ground Road. But if you plan to visit, you may want to hurry. It seems like the tramping ground is disappearing. A few decades ago, the circle was almost 50 feet across; today it is less than half that, and the salinity levels have dropped enough to allow sparse patches of grass to grow.

Now, as for all the other unusual "Devil" places mentioned at the beginning of this episode, most are rather benign . . . even bland. Seven Devils and Kill Devil Hills are nice little towns. The Devil's Branch is a stream in Northampton County. The Devil's Tater Patch, the Devil's Courtyard, and the Devil's Chimney are mountain peaks or hiking trails (or both). The Devil's Head is a unique rock on Exclamation Point Trail in Chimney Rock and appears to have a face.

That leaves the Devil's Rock and the Devil's Stairs. The Devil's Rock is . . . well, a rock. Located off State Road 1131 in what used to be known as Largo in Warren County, there is an indentation in the rock that resembles a left foot. It is slightly larger than a human foot. Mirroring the Devil's Rock in the community of Flat Rock in Lancaster County, South Carolina, there is a matching right foot in another rock. The story goes like this . . .

There was a man in Flat Rock who was said to be one of the meanest men ever to walk the earth. Drinking, gambling, fighting, cussing; all the things that were considered sins—until this new, progressive, modern generation. As he reached a certain age, he began to seriously contemplate his own mortality. Looking back on his life, it seemed obvious which direction he was going to go in death. He realized that he didn't want to go to hell, but he also figured heaven would be awfully damn boring. So he devised a plan to avoid going to either one.

When he knew his time was close, he bought as many tacks as he could find. Then he went out to the rock for which Flat Rock was named, and scattered the tacks all around. He covered them all up with leaves and waited. Soon the devil himself appeared on top of Flat Rock to carry him to the other side.

The man said he was ready and the devil could have him. The devil stepped down off the rock and right onto some of the man's tacks. As pain shot through its foot, the devil howled and, with one foot still on Flat Rock, jumped as high as he could, leaving a right footprint in South Carolina. The story goes that he landed in Largo, leaving his left footprint there.

His plan worked. The devil never returned to claim the man's soul, and heaven certainly wasn't going to take him. It is said that his ghost walks the earth to this day, traveling back and forth between the two rocks, laughing all the while.

The Devil's Stairs is a rock formation near Warrensville, North Carolina. Unlike the other "Devil" formations in North Carolina, the Devil's Stairs are man-made. In 1914, the Norfolk and Western Railroad intended to extend its track through Ashe County. They needed rock, so they blasted it from an area just outside Warrensville, next to Buffalo Creek. When they were finished, what was left resembled four large steps, each about 12 feet high.

The Devil's Stairs got their name because at least one African American worker was killed by a blast of dynamite. Over the next few days, the other workers found bits of the man in the surrounding woods. Soon after this, people claimed to see and hear his ghost near the site of the blast.

Not even a year later, a woman climbed up on one of the steps and threw her newborn child onto the rocks of the Buffalo Creek. A few days later, fishermen claim to have heard a baby's cries coming from the waters of the creek.

But the hauntings of the Devil's Stairs go back much further than 1914.

The earliest European settlers to the area learned that the indigenous Native Americans knew the area was haunted, and steered clear of it at all costs; however, they never learned the exact reason why, and there have been plenty of modern apparitions seen in the area. Most of them are hitchhikers, but, unlike other hitchhiker apparitions, these don't take "no" for an answer.

Just a few years after the stairs were blasted into the side of the mountain, a man was headed home well after nightfall. While the automobile thrived in the larger cities, it would not be widely available to rural America for another decade or so. The man was traveling by horseback.

His horse spooked as the man passed the stairs, but he kept it under control. A bright moon was out, so the man could see his surroundings easily. No one else was around. Suddenly he felt someone "land" on the back of his horse and wrap their arms around him. The arms were hairy.

Not hairy like a hairy man ... but covered in fur like a werewolf or a Bigfoot. This time the horse did bolt, and, although the man was terrified to know what was on the horse with him, it took all of his concentration just to hang on to his horse. It wasn't until they reached the Oak Grove Church, nearly half a mile away, that the man was able to calm the horse. At that point he realized that whatever the creature was was finally gone.

Over the years, several other riders in the area reported similar incidents. And the strange occurrences didn't stop with the introduction to the automobile.

One story from the '50s or '60s tells of a preacher driving home on a dark, rainy night. He saw a hitchhiker near the stairs and stopped to pick him up. The hitchhiker said nothing but accepted the ride. He wore a long, black trench coat with a hood that he never lowered. The preacher tried to strike up a conversation with the man, but he remained silent. The preacher tried to get a look at the man's face, but he could not see past the hood. The stranger never said a word. He just stared straight ahead into the storm. Until he didn't.

The stranger finally turned slowly to look at the preacher. When he did, the preacher didn't see a human face. Whatever the creature was had red, glowing eyes, each as big as a man's fist. The shocked preacher slammed on the brakes, but before he could get the car stopped, the stranger vanished.

Many other people up until this very day have reported driving past the stairs, looking in their rearview mirror, and seeing someone sitting in the back seat ... only to have the intruder disappear just as quickly.

DAN'S STORY

I first visited the infamous Devil's Tramping Ground (DTG) in 2010 for the original iteration of *Carolina Haints*, the video blog. Upon revisiting the videos, I'm thankful they've been removed from YouTube. As a filmmaker, I'm embarrassed by the poor quality of the videos, but as *Carolina Haints* has developed into the podcast and now this book, I can look back with some fondness on those initial concepts.

I traveled to the DTG with my father, who was living in fairly close proximity to it at the time. I think he was just as happy and intrigued to be going there for the first time as I was. I don't know how long he's been familiar with the tales of the DTG, but for myself, being a voracious collector and reader of folklore books, this was a trip for which my excitement couldn't be contained.

Finding the DTG was surprisingly easy, thanks to numerous sources found on Google. While it's commonly listed as being in Siler City, it's actually *near* Siler City, in the community of Bear Creek, in the southwestern region of Chatham County. In Bear Creek, there's a little area of note called Harper's Crossroads where there's

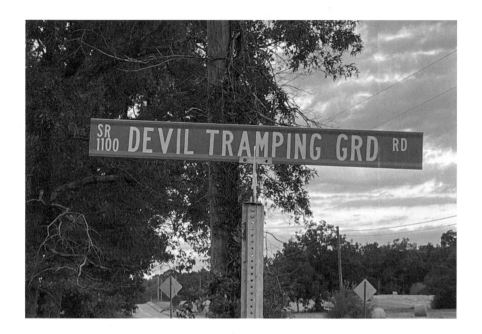

a small gas station and grill. It's located at the intersection of State Highway 902 and Siler City Glendon Road. Nearby, there's another road sign that reads "Devil Tramping Grd Rd," which was how we knew we were on the right track.

To the best of my memory, there's a well-defined dirt path leading into the woods from a worn parking area on the side of the road. I was concerned about the presence of "No Trespassing" signs at the DTG and, being a law-abiding citizen, wasn't prepared to violate the order; however, I was delighted to find no signs in the vicinity at the time. As I made my way through the tall grass and sandy ground, I was on the lookout for snakes and even other folks. I was very aware that this was a common hangout for people wanting to get a firsthand look at the supernatural; "weirdos" like me.

While I didn't find any weirdos, I certainly saw the handiwork of weirdos. One of the first things I found was an old, gray, rotted-looking pillow or blanket that was tied together with a rope and was hanging approximately 30 feet from a tree branch. Part of me wanted to cut down the thing and look inside, but the bigger part of me knows better. If curiosity killed the cat, then I'm fine walking away still curious. In all honesty, it was probably not as interesting as what my overactive imagination could have conceived—some disturbing sight straight out of *The Blair Witch Project*, perhaps a bloody tooth or a bone.

Another image that genuinely scared me into an audible gasp was that of a black figure on a nearby tree. When I first encountered the DTG, it was right before dusk, in those dim twilight minutes before total darkness. I had decided to briefly explore some of the woods just outside the circle when my wandering eyes passed by the figure of a man lit up by my rapidly dying flashlight. I don't know what my excited brain must've thought at first glimpse. Perhaps it was the visage of the devil himself, coming to trample the ground as he's famous for doing.

After I got over the initial shock, I fixed my light upon the tree and approached it for a better look. It was an odd marking of a side profile of a man. It was black, most likely spray paint, but in the dark light it appeared to be burnt bark, charred right onto the wood. There were a few more similar images on other trees nearby, but I was on guard at this point, and they didn't quite get me like this one did.

Now to the infamous circle itself. It's about 20 feet in diameter, to the best of my memory. I'm sure a lot of sources say it's approximately 40 feet, but from my estimation it's not quite so large. And what they say about nothing growing inside it is true! There's no vegetation, no grass, no weeds. I'd be curious to dig around for worms, but the thought didn't occur to me back then.

One thing I was curious about but can't speak much on was the notion that anything left inside the circle will be removed. It was plainly obvious that folks had used the center of the tramping ground for a fire pit. There were still a few charred logs and ashes in the center. Around the center of the circle were three wood stumps placed along the inside of the perimeter, presumably as stools to enjoy the fire. I placed a kerosene lantern near the middle of the circle and came back the next day to find it still in place. While I don't discount the idea that things have been moved outside the circle, I can say this unfortunately wasn't the case on that occasion.

While I can't say I saw or experienced anything supernatural on my visits to the DTG outside of being spooked, I can say the place certainly has a vibe to it. Considering the decades of folklore and oral traditions and writings and even ballads—considering all the visitors who came, either with skeptical minds or hearts full of wonder—it's not hard to imagine all that leaving a mark. Now consider how many times it's likely that someone's come to this spot for nefarious purposes. I'm not aware of any satanic rituals or animal sacrifices or anything like that, but if there ever was a place that would seem to invite that element, the Devil's Tramping Ground would be it.

It's been several years since I've ventured out to that property, but I recently spoke with a friend of mine who works for the Chatham County Sheriff's Office, and he said that the owners of the property have since placed numerous "No Trespassing" signs in an effort to keep folks out. During my visits, I remember seeing only "No Smoking" signs posted. I think it's fair to say that nowadays if you plan on visiting, you should probably try to contact the owners first—or be damn sure not to set the woods on fire.

CHAPTER 11

Legends of Payne Road

Rural Hall, North Carolina

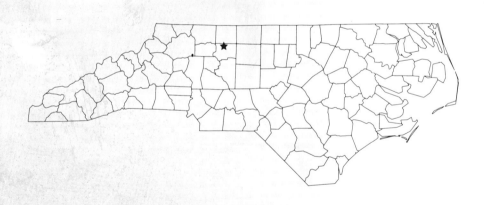

PODCAST • SEASON 2 • EPISODE 13
(February 22, 2019)

It's hard to believe, with all the construction going on seemingly *everywhere*, that North Carolina is known as the "Good Roads State"; however, there are certain roads in this state where drivers should use caution when traveling.

Earlier in this book we covered Lydia's bridge (in "Lydia, the Hitchhiking Ghost"), where the ghost of a tragic car accident appears under a bridge in Jamestown asking for a ride home ... only to vanish once there. Next to Lydia's bridge, Payne Road in Rural Hall is one of the best-known "haunts" of the Carolinas. Technically, the haunted stretch of road is actually Edwards Road.

Whether Payne Road is haunted or not is a matter of debate, but it certainly is one of the state's creepiest roads. It's long and dark, lined with decaying buildings and littered with winding curves.

There are numerous versions of the history of Payne Road. The first concerns a wealthy landowner named Edward Payne (or Payne Edwards, depending on who's telling the story). Payne built Payne Plantation, overlooking one of the valleys in the Rural Hall area. He owned many slaves and treated them with extreme brutality.

He also had four daughters of whom he was extremely protective, so, as you may imagine, he wasn't very pleased when his oldest and unwed daughter became pregnant. But when he found out that the father was one of his very own slaves, he lost his mind. He cursed God himself and turned to devil worship. Of course, the next thing he did was savagely sacrifice the child's father to his newfound deity.

When he then found out his youngest daughter was also consorting with his slaves, he went on a maddening rampage. He murdered his family and set fire to the plantation, killing most of the slaves in the process.

Another story tells of a 1930s-model Ford hot rod racing down Payne Road. When the driver got to the spot where the old Payne Plantation stood, he lost control and crashed. As the bystanders rushed to the man's aid, the car burst into flames, slowly roasting the driver trapped inside.

Drivers today sometimes report being followed by a car with round headlights, just like the old Ford's. When they reach the spot where the man crashed, the ghost car vanishes from sight.

Another story tells of a barn on Payne Road where teenagers would go and make out. The owner of the barn was a Satan worshipper and would chase the kids out whenever he found them on his property. One night, after prom, two kids never returned home. Their parents called their friends and learned that they were all partying out at the Payne Road barn. The parents drove out to look in the barn, and there they found the teenagers hanging from the rafters, still in their formal attire.

In a fourth story, Edward Payne is not a plantation owner but a simple farmer with four daughters. It was not a happy marriage, and he often argued with his wife. One night, after a particularly nasty fight, the man decided that the root of all his problems was his kids. He overpowered his wife in the living room and tied her to a chair. He then went upstairs and brought his eldest girl down. He told her to "kiss your mother good night," and as she leaned forward, he slit her throat with a large carving knife. His second and third daughters met the same fate. But when he brought down the youngest, infant daughter, he couldn't bring himself to do the deed. Instead, he decided he would throw her in the well. The mother struggled and finally broke free of her restraints. She ran after them and snatched the baby from her husband's hands. They fought over the child, and the man chopped the woman's head clean off with the knife and then threw his daughter in the well. With his task done, he hanged himself in the barn. I'm not sure about that version. It seems a little too much like a Violent Femmes song to me (Note: "Country Death Song").

Claims about Payne Road are as numerous as the legends behind it. Some say that if you stop your car on the bridge beside the old house and turn the engine off, it won't restart. Others claim that just driving over the bridge is enough to induce car troubles that linger far after visiting the bridge.

Some say that if you stand on the bridge and whistle "Dixie," you will see the ghostly image of the farmer who hanged himself there. Reports of orange orbs coming from the cemetery are also common, and lesser claims of misty, ghostly figures and phantom dogs have been heard.

So, which legend is the truth? Perhaps none of them. But there was indeed an old farmhouse that sat along one of the road's sharpest curves. And near this farmhouse is the infamous bridge and an old cemetery. Was there really a plantation owner named Edward Payne? There are no records to indicate as much. Did a farmer really kill his family there? Doubtful. The old house that once stood there would be the type of farmhouse to match that story, but most people believe that this story was borrowed from the tragic 1929 Lawson family murders, which happened only 5 miles away.

Even if all the myths behind Payne Road are pure fantasy, the place has seen more than its fair share of documented deaths. Over the years, several people have been murdered in the area, including an alleged prostitute who was reportedly picked up from Winston-Salem by several young men in 1992. She was later found tied to a tree near the infamous farmhouse. She had been raped, tortured, and finally stabbed to death.

Another well-documented case is the suicide of Milus Frank Edwards, who lived in the farmhouse in the mid-1950s. Edwards had four other siblings, *all* of whom had committed suicide. One day, the seventy-three-year-old man parked his truck by one of the sheds near the farmhouse and then proceeded to carry out one of the most dramatic suicides the Triad has ever seen. Edwards kept dynamite in that shed. He fetched himself a stick and climbed into the bed of the pickup. He then lit the stick of dynamite and placed it in his mouth.

Kaboom!

It's not that unusual for a rural area to have seen death over the years, but no one can deny the dramatic ways that people have died on Payne Road. For many, this lends credence to the fact that the place is haunted . . . or cursed.

Today the old farmhouse has burned to the ground, and the original bridge has been replaced by a culvert.

DAN'S STORY

Late one night while working on this book, I decided, what the hell—I would go out and do some research on my own. One of the great things about *Carolina Haints* for me is that it affords me the purpose to do some of the things I've always wanted to do. While driving down a haunted, legendary, infamous country road in the middle of the night sounds like great fun to me, I'd never just go do it for the sake of doing it. But since there's a chapter to be written, well, by God, I now had an excuse.

I arrived in Rural Hall close to 1:00 a.m., and my initial impression in the dark was that it's a pretty little town with some interesting things to see and that it might be a nice place to live. As I turned right onto Edwards Road, I couldn't help but notice a brick building that had the words "Payne and Sons" painted on the side. "This must be the place," I said to myself.

As I rode down the legendary Payne Road in the middle of the night, listening to creepy music, which has been featured on episodes of *The Carolina Haints Podcast*, I couldn't help but feel like I was living an episode of the show myself. I was immediately greeted with fog upon turning onto Edwards Road, which was not something I had encountered the entire trip up to this point. It wasn't a particularly cold night, even as the end of winter rapidly approached. It wasn't raining either, so for me the fog took on a mysterious quality.

Shortly after turning onto the road, I passed by a creepy, old-looking cemetery that sat not too far off the road. It occurred to me that there weren't too many houses close to the road. Perhaps more homes sat farther back off the road, but that would've been hard to determine since the road was so incredibly dark. Using only the illumination of my headlights and what little bit of moonlight I could get, it almost felt that my headlights, even on their brightest setting, were just being consumed by the darkness. There was plenty of fog in the road—not enough to make it difficult to drive, but certainly noticeable.

I found the road to be a bit more winding than what I had expected for this area. I think the windiness helps the road take on a peculiar quality of anticipation; not necessarily a dreadful feeling, but one of curiosity. I didn't expect to see or

encounter anything evil or supernatural, but it was more like the feeling you might get while driving down the road leading to your favorite haunted attraction. I was excited to finally be doing this, and the very thought of putting myself in this situation alone at night, enveloped in darkness, had my senses in a heightened state of awareness.

Near the county line between Forsyth County and Stokes County, there was a clearing in the woods where a house sits, and in the distance you can see some small rolling mountains. Perhaps it was Hanging Rock State Park, a great hiking destination. While the hills loomed in the background, in the foreground were a symphony of skid marks in the roadway, each seeming to tell their own story. It was obvious from the numerous skid marks that plenty of people had taken this curvy country road way too fast.

My ears popped as I continued down the dark roadway; not exactly what I would've expected, even as far north as Stokes County. Soon I approached the stop sign that brought me to the intersection of Edwards and Payne Road. I used my flashlight to try to find a street sign to confirm where I thought I was. This was useless, since there was no sign to be read. I had to resort to using Google Maps to verify where I was. I decided to turn right onto Payne Road, leading out toward Friendship Road, where Payne Road becomes Bolejack Road.

Immediately upon making the turn I was hit with a thick bank of fog; the earlier fog I encountered was nothing compared to this—and although it wasn't planned, my trip was made on a full-moon night. It was bright as hell, and the moonbeams reflected beautifully over the foggy open fields, shining brilliantly through the branches of trees that lined the adjacent fields. The thick fog took on a glowing blue hue as the full moon helped set the perfect ambience.

I drove all the way to Bolejack Road and turned around and came all the way to the other end at NC 66, turning around once again in the parking lot of Friends Mart. I had encountered only one other driver the whole time. As I made my way back, I couldn't help but notice a number of really old and creepy tobacco barns that seemed to line the roadway. I scanned from side to side, trying to imagine where the prostitute was murdered or where the man had committed suicide with a stick of dynamite.

Driving back once again to the other side, to the initial stretch of Payne—which I found to be the creepiest—I slowed down, rolled down my windows, and tried to immerse myself in it as much as I could. I was soon eating my words about it being a warm night, but the cold air just helped add to the experience. I'm used to working third shift, so driving around in the middle of the night is not uncommon for me. I'm from a very rural area originally, similar to this part of the state, and honestly, Payne Road isn't that unfamiliar. It's not unlike any of the many country roads I've traversed in my lifetime. The difference is, those roads don't have the legends associated with them that Payne Road does. It adds a creepy vibe that

someone like me appreciates; someone who would come out here all alone in the middle of a chilly, foggy, moonlit night.

Coming back down Edwards Road and into town was fairly uneventful. I pulled down the driveway of the cemetery, which was blocked by a closed gate. While driving back, it did occur to me that I was perhaps in a bit of danger, but not from anything supernatural. Given the crazy amount of skids on the road, I counted myself lucky that I encountered only one other soul on the road that night and that they didn't come crashing into me. Maybe creating skids is what the kids do around here for fun, but I wasn't about to be the moron who didn't learn from the stories about Payne Road.

My whole trip from one end of Edwards Road to Payne Road and back took about forty minutes. As I continued back toward home, still listening to creepy music in the dark, I couldn't help but feel like I was experiencing the legend firsthand. Prior to embarking on the short journey to Payne Road, I let my research team know where I was going, and asked them to please make sure my story got weaved into the legend, just in case I didn't make it back. I've often remarked to friends that if I were to ever die on the side of the road, I wouldn't want some sort of makeshift floral marker but, rather, would love to be remembered as a legend—a roadside ghost who appears to travelers on cold, foggy nights. As I departed the infamous Payne Road, I felt that there, perhaps better than anywhere, had the potential to fulfill that wish. I'm glad to report that I made it back home safe and sound.

CHAPTER 12

Korner's Folly: The Strangest House in America

Kernersville, North Carolina

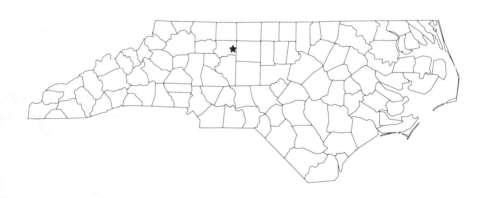

PODCAST • SEASON 1 • EPISODE 9
(December 29, 2017)

In 1878, Jule Korner was twenty-six years old when he decided to build a house at 413 South Main Street in his hometown of Kernersville, North Carolina. It was going to be his home, his office, his art studio, and a way to display his interior-design work. Completed in 1880, the house was immediately ridiculed by the locals because its odd structure and floor plan drastically increased the construction costs. Neighbors began calling the house Korner's Folly (pronounced "Kerner"). Jule liked the name and put the name on a sign in the front yard soon after. Korner's Folly has been called America's Strangest House.

With a moniker like that, it's pretty easy to imagine that comparisons have been made between Korner's Folly and the famous Winchester House in San Jose, California, but they're quite different. Sarah Winchester had been driven mad by the guilt of her family's arms business. She believed that the dead would eventually come to exact their revenge from her, and she built her house haphazardly to prevent them from finding her: stairs that go nowhere, doors that open to walls, rooms within rooms, etc. Korner's Folly was built intentionally and deliberately. There are no two rooms inside Korner's Folly that are identical, and today, people are amazed at Jule's insight and ingenuity.

The house stands three stories tall, but there are seven different levels inside the home, spanning from the cellar to the attic. The home has fifteen fireplaces, but Jule was terrified of fire, and none of them have ever been lit with real fire; instead he had them fit with Franklin stoves. He permitted smoking only in a room lined with tile and built to be fireproof. The ceilings vary from less than 6 feet in some rooms to soaring 25 feet. Jule Korner built his home to be a visual experience.

Some windows extend upward to rooms on the floor above, with neither of them opening. Cubbyholes and trapdoors exemplify Victorian architecture, although Jule often rebelled against Victorian attitudes. When he renovated part of the house to host parties, he built "kissing corners" as an affront to the Victorian authoritarian views of the day. The corners were small closets, just big enough for two people.

Jule also designed a unique air-conditioning system using tunnels built under the floors. Square pieces of wood embedded into the walls and floors, and special pivoting windows could be positioned to allow air flow through the house. A revolving window covers a huge hole that lets air circulate from the stairway 10 feet below.

In addition to making the house his home, Jule also ran his furniture and interior-design business from the house. He was a savvy businessman, making his living in advertising and interior design, but he was also an entrepreneur of several different business opportunities. Some years before building Korner's Folly, he was commissioned by the Blackwell Tobacco Company to create a series of advertisements. Jule, under the pseudonym of Reuben Rink, created America's first national advertising campaign with the Bull Durham Bull. The original Bull Durham was an anatomically correct bull. Soon after the campaign began, recognizing the strategic value of controversy, Jule wrote to a local newspaper pretending to be a woman who was offended by the pictures. Then he wrote his own response to the letter, saying that without the genitals, "you'd think it was merely a cow."

Utilizing his design skills, Korner designed many of the pieces of furniture throughout the house. When the pieces were too large to fit through the doors or up the narrow staircases, he had them built in the room where they would reside.

In 1886, Jule married Polly Alice Masten, the daughter of Forsyth County sheriff Mathias Masten. After their marriage, Jule made several changes around the house to transform it from a bachelor pad into a family home.

Polly Korner . . . or, rather, Alice Korner, as she preferred to be called . . . was a very talented seamstress and spent much of her time with local embroidery and women's groups. She served as president of the Needlework Guild of America in 1910.

The Korners also operated Kernersville's first public library from the home.

Together they had two children and Bob. Jule Gilmer Korner Jr. was born in 1887, and Allie Dore Korner in 1889.

And Bob? As unusual as Korner's Folly is, it seemed only fitting that the Korner children had a unique pet as well; Bob was their pet raccoon.

Alice Korner founded the Juvenile Lyceum or Children's Lyceum, where children ages seven to thirteen were invited to create, rehearse, and perform at Korner's Folly. More than forty children attended the first meeting on April 3, 1896, prompting Jule to turn his billiard room on the top floor into Cupid's Park Theater. To musically support their plays, Alice Korner started the town's first orchestra to play in the theater. The theater got its name from eight Cupid-themed murals painted by famous German artist and close family friend Caesar Milch. The Korners assisted the children in producing these performances, and the entire community was invited to attend. Today, Cupid's Park Theater is still used by local performing-arts groups.

The most popular room in the house may be the ballroom on the second floor. During intermissions, patrons of the theater mingled there and enjoyed refreshments.

Korner's Folly. Photo by Michael Blevins,
courtesy of Korner's Folly Foundation

On Easter Day in 1880, Jule opened the house and invited all of his
family and neighbors to tour Korner's Folly. Although it had officially opened,
he never considered the building to be truly complete. He was constantly
modifying and changing things around the house, and when he died he had
a blueprint of more renovation plans lying on his drawing table.

Jule died in the house on Thanksgiving Day 1924. He was survived by
his wife and two children. Polly Alice Korner died in 1934.

After Jule's wife died, Korner's Folly fell into a state of disrepair. Several
attempts were made to revive the structure; it was a funeral parlor for a
while and, at one point, was also an antique store. During this time, it was
claimed that the furniture would sometimes be moved overnight. The house
was then leased out as rental property for a while, until one resident
damaged parts of the interior. There was then talk of turning the home into
a restaurant before local residents decided enough was enough. Nearly
thirty families, many of them relatives of the Korners, joined together to
purchase the property and have it placed on the National Register of Historic
Places. Eventually their efforts lead to the Korner's Folly Foundation, a
nonprofit organization established as an ongoing attempt to restore and
maintain the unique home.

The ghosts of Korner's Folly don't seem to be haunting it as much as they're simply still living there, content with the memories of the past and happy to entertain guests. While volunteers rarely experience anything unusual, many visitors have often reported that they feel like they are being watched.

One Kernersville resident shared experiences from when his grandmother was a housekeeper on the property. She relayed to him that she heard distinct footsteps descending the staircase even though no one else was inside.

One community theater group that uses Cupid's Park for rehearsals has reported the lights mysteriously turning on and off by themselves.

A repairman was working on the air-conditioning unit in the theater when he felt someone tap him three times lightly on his hat. When he turned to see who was there, he found that he was alone. The man immediately left the building and has refused to ever come back. He even abandoned his tools on the way out.

More than one passerby has claimed to see a little girl standing on the porch in the evening hours. Tour guides have smelled the persistent odor of cigar smoke through the building, when, of course, smoking is strictly forbidden in the house.

Although *Carolina Haints* is not about ghost hunting, it's hard to ignore that aspect of it when talking about Korner's Folly. The foundation readily embraces the ghost-hunting community, and the building has been available to paranormal investigations. All they ask is that the investigators make a donation toward the renovation efforts.

While some paranormal investigations are about obtaining evidence of the afterlife or debunking bogus or mistaken claims, some investigations can be about creating a mystique. Ghosts can be big business. The Korner's Folly Foundation has recognized that the media hype around paranormal investigations can introduce the property to a larger audience and endear it to its current patrons—free advertising after all.

The North Carolina chapter of the well-known TAPS (the Atlantic Paranormal Society) was the first paranormal team to investigate the house. Bruce Frankel had recently become the new director of the Korner's Folly Foundation and had no idea if the house was haunted or not, and frankly he didn't care; however, being a business owner himself, he identified an opportunity for the location both to acquire additional renovation funds and receive some much-needed publicity. Together with the ghost hunters, they coordinated several newspaper and television interviews, playing to their strengths. On one hand, the TAPS name carried a lot of recognition through the *Ghost Hunters* television program, and on the other hand, Korner's Folly is rich with local history and original furnishings.

The TAPS team investigated the house and at first didn't find very much extraordinary about the location. A rustling noise was heard in the kitchen, along with a couple of unexplained knocks from the same area, electromagnetic field (EMF) fluctuations, and a small flash of light that seemingly appeared out of nowhere, but then the activity started to pick up. At least one investigator claimed to be pushed by an unseen force, and another witnessed the apparition of a woman.

The audio and video tapes were reviewed, and at about the same time that the small flash of light was seen, a little girl's voice could be heard saying, "Peek-a-boo." Later, another investigator switched on her recorder and announced, "Starting EVP session." A man's voice was captured asking, "What is EVP?" The investigator who saw the woman's apparition asked, "What's your name?," and a response is heard: "Annie."

DAN'S STORY

I made my first visit to Korner's Folly a few years ago with my wife. We had just bought a new car at a nearby dealership, and for some reason we had some time to kill. Somehow I talked her into stopping by the strangest house in America for a visit. This was totally not her sort of thing, but I explained to her that we would be covering it for an upcoming episode of *The Carolina Haints Podcast* and that it was haunted. I had spoken with the executive director, Dale Pennington, about the hauntings, and she offered some good resources to check out. But as you've probably gathered from this book, the stories themselves go only so far to satisfy my curiosity. I had to go there and see the place for myself.

My wife is such a trouper; like she's done so many times before, she put my desires ahead of her own, and pretty soon, with a set of new wheels, we pulled into the gravel parking lot on South Main Street in Kernersville. Before you walk in the house, you pay a small admission fee and sit in a little room to watch a video that explains the rules for visitors and some of the house's history. It sounds a bit hokey, but it helps give visitors, especially folks like my wife who knew nothing about the house, a little bit of context before entering. We came at the right time because there were no other visitors to navigate around, and we had the whole house to ourselves—besides, of course, the friendly yet vigilant staff . . . and any ghosts that were present.

To be fair, we stayed for about an hour and a half and never encountered anything that we believed to be paranormal. But unless you're a ghost hunter or a psychic medium, I would never expect to find anything particularly haunting about the place. It's beautiful and old and intricate, but all of that could be found through a Google search or by perusing their website. What you can't get without visiting is the way the place feels, and I suppose that

The Korner Family. Photo courtesy of Korner's Folly Foundation

too is a bit subjective. If you ask this writer, I'd tell you that the place had a pretty heavy feeling to it. Not a dark or ominous feeling, but one of rich history and strong intention.

Every room was meticulously designed, constructed, and eventually remodeled and refurbished with the expressed intention of capturing Jule Korner's vision. I spoke with an employee of the Korner's Folly Foundation, who helped me understand what it's like to work there. Suzanna Ritz is the operations and programs manager and has been in that position for a few years. Suzanna's job is to manage most aspects of visitor services, including admissions, the gift shop, interpretation/signage, and housekeeping, to make sure all visitors have a positive and engaging experience. Another big part of her job is creating and implementing educational and public programming, and she's also responsible for managing the collections: making sure all objects in the house are inventoried, appropriately displayed or stored, and researched.

Suzanna told me that one of the most interesting tidbits of her job is maintaining the less accessible areas of the house. She has the unique honor of changing the HVAC filters located underneath the house, which means she has to open the trapdoors and lower herself under the floor. The first time she did it, she was apprehensive. She said it's very dry and clean down there, with gravel floors and clay walls, and she couldn't help but think of how fitting it was to house the system down there, since Jule Korner himself designed the trapdoors to allow cool air to flow through the house during the warmer months. Suzanna claims she's never experienced anything she would characterize as supernatural and has had only very "normal" experiences there.

It's only natural to visit a haunted house and expect to see a ghost, but honestly, I think I pretty much forgot about the haunted aspect of Korner's Folly and just became immersed in the grandeur. Some of the rooms are truly grand and intricate. I could see myself spending all day moving from corner to corner and wall to wall, examining each and every minute aspect, soaking it all in. Some of the rooms are so small and the doorways are so tight you can hardly fit through them. The place is pretty much a big maze. There are tiny corridors and ventilation shafts, and fireplaces with a network of flues.

Walking through the house, you might stop and think that Jule Korner was either a total engineering genius or a whack job with more money than good sense. While the latter may make for a more entertaining chapter, I must admit that my distinct impression was the former. In fact, as I slowly made my way from room to room, I was in awe of the place; not only the vision, but the dedication put into it. And to be fair, it's not just the initial concept from 1880, but the fact that the house was in a continual state of addition and reconstruction and redesign.

The Little Theater. Photo by Michael Blevins,
courtesy of Korner's Folly Foundation

As if the interior design and planning wasn't enough to impress, stop to think for a moment that just a few decades ago, the place was in shambles and at serious risk of being lost to history. Through the commitment of dedicated citizens and neighbors, the house was restored to its original glory and is now open for all to enjoy. I very much encourage you to go pay a visit and spend some time there enjoying all there is to see and experience—and don't waste your energy looking for haints. I know this book is about ghost stories, and don't worry, there's plenty here, but there's so much to be impressed with about Korner's Folly that the ghosts themselves seem trite.

CHAPTER 13

The Specters of Mordecai House

Raleigh, North Carolina
Cary, North Carolina

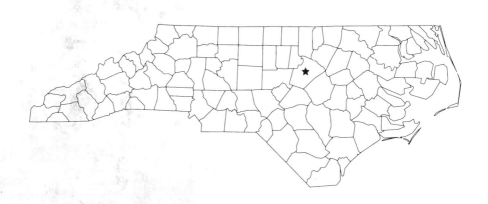

PODCAST • SEASON 3 • EPISODE 10
(January 17, 2020)

The Mordecai House, built in 1785, is the oldest residence in Raleigh that still stands on its original foundation. The house currently sits in the Mordecai Historic Park. But when it was originally built, the simple farmhouse was intended to be the centerpiece of Joel Lane's 5,000-acre plantation. Colonel Joel Lane is considered the father of Raleigh, since he sold the county the 1,000-acre lot where the city would be founded.

The Mordecai House was inherited by Joel's son Henry in 1785. Henry, in turn, had two daughters: Margaret and Ann. In 1817, Margaret married Moses Mordecai. Mordecai was a lawyer and a politician. In fact, he came from a long line of prominent North Carolinians. As well as being lawyers and politicians themselves, his ancestors were also educators and activists, and his grandfather was among the first group of Jewish immigrants to settle in America. Moses and Margaret took over the house and had three children of their own.

Just four years into their marriage, in 1821, Margaret died and Moses married her sister, Ann, almost immediately. Moses and Ann had big plans for the old family home. He hired a well-known area architect to renovate and expand the house. William Nichols was the architect of the North Carolina State House as well as the Alabama and Mississippi State Houses. Nichols transformed the simple farmhouse into a Greek Revival mansion and gave it the moniker of Mordecai House. Around this time, Moses also decided to change the pronunciation of his name. He changed it from Mordec-EYE (as it is spelled) to Morde-KEY.

Joel Lane and Moses Mordecai were both wealthy slave owners, but the Civil War stripped Mordecai of both his slaves and his fortune. Later generations survived by slowly selling off the 5,000-acre property, one piece at a time.

The family managed to keep control of the house until 1967. A group of developers offered to purchase the property, but when the public learned that they planned to raze the house and turn it into a parking lot, concerned citizens stepped in. They pressured the city and the Raleigh Historic Development Commission to purchase Mordecai House and enter it into the National Register of Historic Places.

To recoup their cost, the historical commission wanted to open the Mordecai House up for tours. The house, however, was in a serious state of disrepair. During the renovations, construction workers noticed several peculiar things happening on the property.

Once the house was open to the public, there was no denying it . . . the Mordecai House was haunted. Many paranormal events began to be reported by the housekeepers and the public alike, but according to one caretaker, it's after all the tourists leave for the day that things get particularly interesting. "I saw objects move," he says. "I heard footsteps upstairs, but I was alone." However, he adds, "You get used to it."

The Mordecai House is believed to be haunted by at least two women. Some believe that Margaret Lane haunts the house and can be seen walking around the house wearing a long, black skirt and a white blouse.

And the ghost of Moses's granddaughter, Mary Willis Mordecai Turk, is also seen in the house. Mary lived from 1858 to 1937. She can sometimes be heard playing the piano and is occasionally seen as a full-body ghost in a gray nineteenth-century dress; however, witnesses usually see a thin gray mist hovering near the piano.

There was another historic home only 15 miles from Mordecai House in Cary. The fate of High House is quite different from that of Mordecai, but its story is no less interesting.

In 1760, Tingnal Jones built a house for his son, Fanning Jones. The house dominated the landscape. It was built on a hill at the highest part of the road and was the only two-story house in the general area. It soon became known as "the High House." By the time Fanning Jones moved away from North Carolina in 1822, the road itself was called High House Road.

During the time that Fanning Jones occupied the house, High House was the party house of Cary. Fanning hosted horse races on the 1,200-acre property, drawing in sportsmen, gamblers, prostitutes, and an abundance of alcohol. Of course, such an establishment also attracted its share of violence. These horse races would often result in hard feelings, fistfights, and even gunshots. One story tells of two men who were in love with the same girl. One day, while everyone was distracted watching a horse race, one of the men pulled the girl away from the other spectators and strangled her to death before anyone noticed.

Many believe that she is *the* ghost of High House.

In the 1830s, Nathaniel Green Alford purchased the house and the land. Nathaniel's daughter Perninan and her husband, Robert Williams, took over the property on his passing. This was all well before the Civil War, and a 1,200-acre property needed many slaves to keep it running. The slaves claimed the house was haunted by the spirit of a woman, but no one really believed them.

In 1850, Perninan and Robert had a son they named William . . . that's right, William Williams. They had two slave boys about William's age, and they often played and did their chores together. One evening, when little Willie was eleven years old, he was out in the orchard gathering apples with the slave children. His parents were attending evening church service. He turned and looked toward High House and saw a woman walking in the yard. From that distance, Willie couldn't make out who it was, but he assumed that his parents had returned. He ran to the house with a few of the other boys, but no one was there. An hour later, when his parents finally returned, an excited Willie told them his story. His father dismissed it and sent Willie to his room.

Willie would see the ghost at least two more times before the Civil War. One summer evening he was playing in the front yard with his slave friends when she appeared just a few feet away. She opened the front gate and walked through it toward the old horse racetrack. Willie ran inside to get his father, but when they got back outside the other children said that she had just vanished. Now, Robert Williams was a stern man. He had already told Willie that there was no ghost, and he meant that there was no ghost. Thankfully, the next time Willie encountered the ghost, his mother was with him. Willie was in the workroom, again playing with his friends, while his mother quilted a comforter. Suddenly they all heard a loud commotion in the room above them. Willie's mother called for some of the adult slaves to investigate, and of course nothing was there. Robert Williams arrived back home later that evening, and they told him what had happened.

"Enough is enough!" he declared. "There is no ghost!" He forbade them to mention the subject again.

Then came the day when Robert Williams saw the ghost for himself. It was cotton-picking time, and Robert had just gotten in from a long day in the fields. He was tired and cranky, and he just wanted to rest for a while. Suddenly a woman walked through the hall, popped her head in the door, and turned to go upstairs. Robert thought it was his daughter Roxanna trying to scare him, and he called her back into the room. When the woman ignored him and continued up the stairs, Robert got very angry. He walked out to the base of the stairs and demanded that Roxanna present herself that very moment. Roxanna and her mother were in the kitchen. When they heard Robert yelling, they knew he was mad. They both came out of the kitchen to see what was going on. Of course, that left Robert bewildered. He searched the upstairs himself, but there was no one there.

He still would not admit that there was a ghost in the house, but he was starting to believe that "something" was going on.

Robert Williams died in 1861. A few years later, Willie Williams married a girl and moved to her hometown of Raleigh. Roxanna also married and stayed in High House with her mother. Toward the turn of the century, William's wife died, and he moved back to High House with his four children. More than thirty years had passed, and William had put all thoughts of the ghost out of his head, but one day his own daughter came running to him, saying that she saw a woman out in the front yard who had vanished. This brought back all of William's childhood memories. Soon after this, he packed up the entire family and moved to Biscoe, North Carolina.

Once again, High House sat vacant.

I mentioned that the fate of High House was very different from that of the Mordecai House. After Mordecai House sat abandoned, it was finally saved by the city of Raleigh and restored. Such was not the destiny of High House.

One night in the early 1900s, Leander Williams, one of Willie's cousins who still lived in Cary, had an odd dream. He had spent a lot of time at High House as a child, and something in the dream told him that there was a great treasure buried beneath the hearth at the old house. Leander woke dazed and confused. He told his mother about the dream, and she paled. She had had the exact same dream. They immediately rushed to the abandoned house . . . only to find that someone had beaten them there. The hearth had very recently been torn apart brick by brick.

Leander's mother told her friends about their experience, and word of the treasure of High House quickly spread. By the mid-1900s, the house had been completely demolished by fortune hunters. If anyone ever found a treasure, they never admitted it.

DAN'S STORY

Several years ago I asked Jeff Cochran to write a special episode of the podcast about the multiple hauntings of the theaters of Greensboro. At the time, Wreak Havoc Productions was holding the Wreak Havoc Horror Film Festival at the historic Carolina Theatre of Greensboro. Through our association I befriended a member of their marketing team, Gigi Galdo, who had a great idea to host a paranormal lock-in night at the theater, a notoriously haunted building. The idea was to take guests on a tour of the building, highlighting the various ghostly tales throughout, and then let them take part in a paranormal investigation. I was asked to give a reading of *The Carolina Haints Podcast* in front of a live audience. It went well and we got an interesting episode of the show out of it.

This association with the Carolina Theatre eventually led to me directing a short film for them called *Ghosts of the Carolina*. It was the first film I've ever directed without producing, and not only was it a joy to work on, but the thing turned out pretty decent! Anyway, Jeff and I were asked back a second year to do another live offering of *Carolina Haints* at the theater. I can't speak for Jeff, but I had an excellent time. The reading went well and connected with the audience, and we got a video out of it that we published just in time for Halloween. Jeff and I got to hang out, drink a few beers, eat some snacks, and hang out with some friends, and I got my Tarot cards read by a lovely and uncomfortably accurate medium. We also met Nelson Nauss.

Nelson is a member of the Ghost Guild, a paranormal investigative team out of Raleigh. While ghost hunting isn't my thing, Nelson was a nice guy and we had a good bit to talk about. As you might imagine, a paranormal investigator and the host of a storytelling show devoted to ghosts and folklore have a lot in common. Reluctantly, I accompanied Nelson's team on a few missions throughout the building. The Carolina Theatre has some truly great ghost stories worthy of its own chapter (which we may get to someday); however, I spent most of the night just wandering around the darkened corridors of this beautiful, old building, hoping to have some sort of experience without the provocation of an investigation. Unfortunately, no specter appeared before me that night, and the investigation failed to yield credible results, but I stayed in contact with Nelson.

When it came time to research this chapter about the Mordecai House, it turns out my meeting Nelson was fortuitous. We had made arrangements with him and the director of the Mordecai Historic Park to tour the location and all the buildings on its grounds. As with so much of this book, plans to explore in-depth, in person, were waylaid by the infamous COVID-19. Plans to see this place with my research crew have been postponed indefinitely; however, Nelson agreed to tell me a bit about his research into Mordecai. The Ghost Guild has a contract to be the site's exclusive paranormal investigative team. If Nelson Nauss couldn't tell me what I needed to know, nobody could.

"The Ghost Guild, Inc., is a registered nonprofit organization composed of folks from varying backgrounds but that all share a love for history, science, and the unexplained. We generally seek to investigate locations of political, military, and cultural historical significance," Nelson explains. He said that when the contract for an exclusive investigative team opened up at the Mordecai Historic Park, "we applied, along with many other teams, and went through a rigorous interview process. Josh Ingersoll, director for Mordecai

Historic Park, said that we were selected because of our science-based approach in conducting our investigations. He also appreciates that we don't label things as 'evidence' when we share our data. We always encourage our audience, their guests, to think critically in making their own conclusions." I'm sure it didn't hurt that "Mordecai has always been a location that is near and dear to our hearts," he added.

The Ghost Guild has investigated Mordecai Historic Park a total of twelve times, averaging about four per year since 2017. We often try to schedule our investigations around significant events. For example, a local theater company, MOJOAA, hosts an interactive performance called Escape to Freedom, which leads the audience through the experience of antebellum slave life. We have participated in this experience and followed it with an overnight investigation. Most recently, we investigated the property over the Christmas holiday, incorporating songs and traditions of the season to see if it might entice the spirits to join along. On one occasion we had Sam Mordecai, an ancestor of Moses Mordecai, join us and bring along some Mordecai family artifacts to see if that would stir up some additional activity.

As you might've imagined, the Mordecai Historic Park has a welcoming attitude about its hauntings and even hosts the annual Haunted Mordecai Festival. According to Nelson, "this festival is a family- and pet-friendly event held on the Mordecai property every year around Halloween. People come from all over to enjoy food, music, games, crafts, costume contests, lantern tours, a haunted trolley tour, and, of course, our annual reveal. In exchange for having exclusive access to investigate Mordecai Historic Park, we present our data, stories, and experiences that we've collected during our investigations of the park. We typically hold three back-to-back presentations on the day of the Haunted Mordecai Festival, and mostly all a full house. We also get to draw one lucky winner to join us for one of our investigations of the park for the following year."

Nelson and his crew have devoted a considerable amount of time, energy, and resources to the park. I wanted to know what was so special about the place to merit all the attention. Nelson said that "generations of family called Mordecai House their home, and that kind of history and energy is what makes this property so special. It is soaked into the foundation and is palpable from the moment you walk in the door. You can feel the energy almost like a warm memory. It embraces you, almost as though you are a part of the family and it is welcoming you home. One of our favorite things about Mordecai is the mystery of the things we can't explain. We have had a similar experience on multiple investigations that we have yet to be able to debunk. We continue

Mordecai House. Photo by Nelson Nauss

to work diligently to try to capture the phenomenon in the act to identify a rational explanation for it. Until then, it continues to elude us."

As you know, paranormal investigations are not my interest in these tales. But as time goes on, and more of these investigations build on the legacy of preexisting legends, it's hard to escape their impact. After a while, it's hard to pick apart what's data and what's folklore. But I wanted to know just how their findings seem to jive with the stories that've been told about this place. Nelson said, "Interpretation of 'potentially paranormal' data is always a tricky subject, especially with audio data. It is rare to have a 100 percent agreement amongst reviewers on what they hear or see. With this in mind, we have the advantage of being able to collect not just one night's worth of data, but numerous nights of data. In the long run, perhaps the combination of various data points from multiple investigations will help to verify and confirm the legends. I wouldn't say our data speaks directly to the legends you may have come across, but it does speak to the history of the family. We often get responses when engaging specific family members directly. One of our investigators is also an empath. In one of our earliest investigations, she had an experience so emotional for her that she had to leave the property. She described what she saw and felt to the assistant director of the Mordecai property, and only then did she learn that the feelings and images she saw were related to the documented loss of a Mordecai child. One of our goals as a team is to connect the history of the locations we investigate with the paranormal activity being reported. In most locations we are able to easily debunk and explain away the things that occur, but Mordecai keeps us on our toes."

CHAPTER 14

The First Ghosts of Salem and the Little Red Man

Winston-Salem, North Carolina

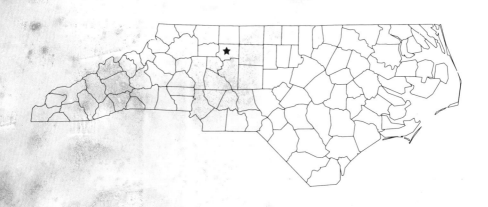

PODCAST • SEASON 1 • EPISODE 8
(December 15, 2017)
AND
PODCAST • SEASON 2 • EPISODE 12
(February 8, 2019)

Winston-Salem is the fifth-largest city in North Carolina, but before 1913 it did not technically exist. Until then, it was two separate townships: Salem and Winston.

The Moravians had, and continue to have, a large presence in Pennsylvania. Moravians are Protestant, and they boast the oldest Protestant church in existence, built in 1457 in Moravia, in the Czech Republic. But the Moravians hold slightly different beliefs than other Protestants. This, coupled with the misconception by some that all Moravians still live like the reenactors at Old Salem, have led to the Moravians being confused with the Quakers, or the Amish, or even the Mormons. The truth is, other than sharing the basic tenets of Christianity, they have very little in common with these other religions.

In 1753, they looked for an area where they could expand. When they found the Piedmont of North Carolina, they felt it was reminiscent of their European homeland. They purchased 100,000 acres of land, more than 150 square miles, or two-thirds of what is now Forsyth County. They called this new land the Wachovia Tract.

About a dozen men came down from the Moravian settlement in Pennsylvania and established the settlement of Bethabara, which was intended to be a temporary location until their capital city of Bethania could be built. Bethania was spared from annexation in 1995 and remains the only continuously active Moravian town in the South.

Other towns soon began to spring up in the Wachovia Tract: Friedberg, Friedland, Hope, and, of course, Salem. One key feature for any permanent settlement is water. Salem was built at the confluence of two prominent creeks, Peters Creek and Salem Creek. The name "Salem" was derived from "Shalom," the Hebrew word for peace. But now I think it's fair to say that *some* of the area's residents have failed to find any peace. Even in the afterlife.

The first known haunt of Salem was George Stockburger, a once-wealthy farm owner who had fallen on bad times. One day, workers at the paper mill found him half dead on the banks of Peters Creek. They called the mill owner, who sent for the town doctor. It was several days before George was strong enough to tell them his story.

You see, in those days the terrain that made up the Wachovia Tract was quite different from modern-day Winston-Salem. Many hills and steep ravines covered much of the area. Caves dotted the walls of many of these ravines. All of these caves have been lost over the years as the ravines were filled in and the ground flattened to make way for ever-expanding construction. But in the late 1700s, Peters Creek had been dammed to create Peters Mill Pond, which fed the Peters Paper Mill. Peters Mill Road (today's Peters Creek Parkway) led to the mill via Peters Mill Bridge at the head of Peters Mill Pond. Yeah, I know, that's a lot of Peter, but it's an integral part of the story—just bear with me.

While Salem was a God-fearing town of peace, the heavily wooded areas outside town were known to be home to all manner of supernatural creatures, including three witches who lived in one of the caves north of Peters Creek.

George Stockburger was a desperate, broken man. He had lost his farm and his family and had gotten himself kicked out of the church. He was at his wit's end. He decided to brave the evil backwoods and visit the witches, who were rumored to be the best soothsayers in the region. He asked them to look into his future. When would things get better for him? Would he ever catch a break?

They did not give him the answer he was hoping for, instead telling him that his future looked bleak.

Deciding to end his life, George threw himself off Peters Mill Bridge, hoping to drown in the waters of Peter Mill Pond, but as soon as he hit the water, he had second thoughts. He struggled to get back to shore, his strength failing him. He claimed that the last thing he remembered before losing consciousness was being pulled out of the water by an unseen entity, which he believed to be divine intervention.

The mill owner took pity on him and gave him a job as the mill's ragman, which was sort of an older form of recycling. George Stockburger worked for the mill until he died. And some say even beyond death.

It is said that after his death, George's disembodied voice could be heard around town calling out the ragman's motto: "Rags for the paper mill, ladies?"

In 1786, Andreas Kremser was a chimney sweep in Salem. He was a kind and playful man who would walk the streets with a red cap perched on his head and cheerfully nod to everyone he met. He especially loved the children and would make an extra effort to play with them and make them smile; however, the church and the community leaders (who were more or less the same people) criticized his chimney-sweeping skills. Salem experienced an epidemic of measles, and the leaders claimed it was due to the frequency and quality of the town's chimney cleanliness.

Kremser was slight of stature and too small to climb some of the chimneys in town. The church thought a larger, more industrious man was needed for the job. Kremser defended himself, saying that the town had too many chimneys for one man to keep up to the standards that the leaders demanded.

He eventually quit chimney-sweeping and worked for a short time in the kitchen of the Brothers House until finding his true calling as a cobbler. For the rest of his life he could be found in his workroom in the Brothers House . . . wearing his favorite little red cap . . . tap-tap-tapping with his shoemaker's hammer.

What is the Brothers House, you ask? Moravian *couples* lived in normal family homes. Everyone else was divided up by their status into choirs. Single men, single women, and widows each lived in their own separate buildings.

The Brothers House, built in 1769, was designed "to withstand time and sorrow," and, indeed, it still stands today, 250 years later. Its walls are extremely thick, and it has four stories: three floors and a basement. The two upper levels were for eating, sleeping, and working. The first floor, called the "first

Single Brother's House. Photo by Zack Fox

basement," contained the kitchen and additional workspace. The rear of the first floor is only about 4 feet high to accommodate the slope of the land.

Below ground is the subbasement, referred to as the "deep cellar." It has a high, vaulting ceiling; it's a gloomy, dark place with no windows. In the late 1700s the only illumination came from candles and lanterns.

In 1786, the brothers built an addition onto their house. As was their custom, the men performed their regular duties during the day, then, after evening worship, they would work on the addition. They often worked well past midnight.

On the night of March 25, 1786, Kremser and several other men decided to work in the deep cellar. It was common practice at the time to dig an undercut at the base of the wall; then the soil above could be brought down quickly and cleanly.

Around 11:30 that night, another brother came into the basement and commented that the overhanging soil looked loose and unstable. The men digging the undercut didn't think there was any danger, and continued working. Around midnight the overhang began to collapse. Everyone scrambled to safety . . . except Andreas Kremser. The wall came down, burying him under a ton of sand, soil, and rock—only his red cap was visible.

The other men worked quickly to free him, and, alarmed by the commotion, other brothers came from upstairs to also help. Kremser was freed as quickly as possible. His leg was clearly broken, but he was conscious and alert, complaining of extreme pain. The doctor did everything he could, but it was soon apparent that Andreas did not have much time left. He passed away only a few hours later.

Kremser was remembered in the many tears that fell that night.

But Kremser's story doesn't end there. Soon after the fatal accident, the other brothers began to hear unusual creaking and knocking noises at night. Whispers of ghosts began to spread among the brothers. The church frowned upon this kind of talk and severely admonished the men. The large building was more than twenty years old and was bound to creak at night due to settling and weather. Besides, the Moravians do not believe in ghosts, but that doesn't mean the ghost didn't believe in them . . .

Before long, it became obvious that these were no ordinary creaks and knocks. At times, the unmistakable tap-tap-tapping of a shoemaker's hammer could be heard. And, on occasion, light footsteps could be heard walking through the halls when no one was there. The frightened men would look at each other and whisper, "There's Kremser." But they were torn. Who or what did they fear more?

A ghost?

Or the church that forbid them from acknowledging it?

As time passed, there was no denying that something unusual was going on in the Brothers House. From time to time, one of the brothers caught a quick glimpse out of the corner of his eye, seeing a flash of red as a figure slipped past a doorway. Of course, when they investigated, no one was there. Eventually, even members of the church leadership began to concede that they may indeed have a specter among their congregation.

Years passed and the brothers found themselves no longer in need of such a large building. They moved out, and the building became the Widows House. Occasional sightings of Kremser continued to be reported from time to time, but the widows enjoyed a good tale, and stories of Kremser and his ghost were talked about often.

When Betsy was just a baby, she became very sick. She recovered from her illness, but the ordeal left her deaf. When she was a bit older, she was at the Widows House spending some time with her grandmother. Being deaf for most of her life, she had never heard about Andreas Kremser. So, as you can imagine, everyone was stunned when she came running into the room to her grandmother, saying that she saw a little man in the hallway and he motioned for her to come to him.

There is a more recent story, or at least recent enough for electric lights to have been installed in the deep cellar. Two men were down there. One was rather skeptically listening as the other man told him the story of the Little Red Man of Old Salem. Suddenly the apparition appeared before them, seemingly as solid as you or I. Thinking that someone was playing a joke on them, the first man motioned to the second and they attempted to grab the figure. They closed in on him and pounced, only to wrap their hands around thin air. A tapping noise made them look behind, where they saw the Little Red Man taunting them from across the room before vanishing completely.

The story finally came to an end when a visiting minister heard the tale and decided to put a stop to Old Salem's ghost once and for all. He strode through the Widows House praying and invoking the Holy Trinity and commanding the spirit of Kremser to rest at peace. Apparently, it worked. There have been no reported sightings since.

And what of the witches talked about in the George Stockburger story?

George Washington took care of them.

During his first term in office, President George Washington vowed to visit all thirteen colonies. He came to Winston-Salem at the beginning of summer 1791. He stayed in the Salem Tavern, which still stands on South

Main Street. Washington was so impressed with the area that he decided to stay an extra day, calling Salem an "oasis in the wilderness."

He spent the extra day touring the region in greater detail. When he and his tour guide reached Peters Mill Bridge, Washington could tell that something was bothering his guide. After questioning the young man, he told the president about the three witches. Washington demanded to be taken to the women.

The man took Washington within sight of the cave where the witches lived, but refused to go any farther. Washington went on alone and entered the witches' cave. A short while later he returned and allegedly told the man, "This was not my first encounter with the supernatural or unholy beings; however, I hope that it is my last."

After the president left Salem, some men went to the caves but found no sign of the witches. For the weeks that followed, strange shrieks and wails could be heard coming from the caves late at night, but the witches were never seen again.

One hundred years after the Wachovia Tract purchase, the population of Salem was still only a couple of hundred people, but between 1800 and 1850 two events took place that made Salem a revolving door of activity. Washington wasn't kidding when he said that he was impressed with Salem. Upon returning to the US capital, he declared that Salem should be one of the post towns of America. The post town project was established to designate layover areas for families moving west, beyond the thirteen colonies.

Washington passed away in 1799. He did not live long enough to see this become a reality, but Thomas Jefferson honored his predecessor's wishes. For the next twenty years, the Great Migration brought a constant flow of wagon trains into Salem—thousands of people a month.

The vast majority of these people did not stay in the area but simply restocked their supplies before heading west; however, if it's true, as many believe, that ghosts need energy to manifest and survive, then Salem certainly saw its share of energy during this time. People of all walks of life traveled its thoroughfares, slept at its inns, and supported its shops.

In addition to the natural caves that once dotted the landscape of Forsyth County, there are also hundreds of forgotten man-made holes all over the state of North Carolina. In 1799, a twelve-year-old boy named Conrad Reed found a shiny rock on his family's farm in Cabarrus County. The family used the rock as a doorstop for a few years until John Reed, the boy's father, decided to show it to a jeweler. The rock, as it turned out, was a 17-pound solid-gold nugget. Not understanding the value of gold, Reed sold the rock to the jeweler for $3.50. It was valued at the time to be worth $3,600.

Thus began America's first gold rush. Over the next few decades, hundreds, if not thousands, of mines were dug across the state in search of the elusive mineral. Nearly all of them have been sealed up, and most have been forgotten to time, but they are still there. Every couple of years the North Carolina Department of Environmental Quality has to deal with the sinkholes that open up when one of them collapses.

Oh . . . and don't feel too sorry for John Reed. Having learned from his mistake, he invested in large-scale mining on his farm. He deposited more than 2,500 ounces of gold before the mine ceased operation. But the Carolina gold rush also caused thousands of people to migrate to and from the area of Salem. Hundreds came in search of North Carolina gold, and many, having made their riches, left the area just as quickly. The end of the North Carolina gold rush coincided very closely with the beginning of the California gold rush, so many of the experienced workers left for California to work new mines.

For those who did decide to stay in the area, very, very few of them were Moravian. And while Salem did not require its residents to be of the Moravian faith, the newly formed Forsyth County decided to establish a town to become its county seat. In 1848, the county purchased land from Salem and formed the town of Winston to accommodate these newcomers.

In 1875 R. J. Reynolds opened his tobacco company in Winston, North Carolina. At that time, the combined population of Winston and Salem was just 443 souls, but both areas would grow and expand, blurring the lines between them. By 1913 the area had grown to 25,000 people, and the two towns officially combined to become Winston-Salem.

By the 1940s, RJR had dozens of old warehouses that dated back to the formation of the company but were no longer in use. The story goes that a group of men were told to clean out and secure the basement of one of these old warehouses. They moved a stack of barrels and were confounded by what they found concealed behind them. A double set of sliding doors were set into the side of the building.

The first question that puzzled them was, Where do they lead? They were underground, after all. And the second unfathomable thought was, What in the world were they used for? The doors were *huge*! They were 12 feet high and 12 feet across—each. They were chained shut and padlocked.

Overcome by curiosity, the men decided to find out what lay beyond the doors. The padlock was extremely old and rusty and fell away easily after they cut it with some bolt cutters.

They opened the doors to find an old, brick-lined mine shaft. They retrieved some flashlights and explored the shaft for several minutes. They saw that numerous smaller side shafts branched off to either side, but they stuck to the main shaft for fear of getting lost in the maze of shafts. Suddenly they began to see other lights down there with them.

At first they panicked, thinking that perhaps a supervisor had caught them somewhere they ought not be. But the lights were in front of them, as well as down some of the side shafts. What could they be?

As they got closer, they saw a dozen or so ghostly miners, the light coming from lamps strapped to their heads. They bustled here and there, working the mine, but paid no attention to the men staring at them. They were covered head to toe in dirt and mud, and by their equipment and dress, the men guessed that they were from the 1830s or '40s (a hundred years before the R. J. Reynolds employees found them), at the height of the Carolina gold rush.

The men ran back to the warehouse basement. They closed the doors and found a new padlock to replace the one that they had cut.

If you've traveled through the heavy-construction area of Business Route 40 lately, you may have noticed a huge arch that looks like part of some giant swing set that marks the boundary between the original towns of Salem and Winston.

DAN'S STORY

I first visited Old Salem Museum and Gardens in 2010 for the original iteration of *Carolina Haints*. Back then, I covered the story of the Little Red Man and was able to take my camera all throughout the Single Brothers House. Of course, I didn't encounter anything I'd characterize as spooky, except for maybe some of the reenactors. But seriously, if you're into history, this is one of the coolest places you can visit in North Carolina. It's like immersing yourself inside a living museum. I've had the good fortune of having visited Old Salem on a number of occasions since then with family members and friends, and the place never disappoints. Whether it's lunch at Salem Tavern or the full ticketed-tour experience, the place is a treasure. Not only have the houses and buildings been restored and kept up to historical specifications, but there's folks dressed in period garb, eager to talk to you about life in the early days of the settlement. There was more than enough to pique my interest without the mention of ghosts.

"God's Acre" Salem Moravian Graveyard.
Photo by Zack Fox

To help fill in some of the gaps, I was able to speak with Blake Stevenson, who's worked for Old Salem for twenty-five years and is currently the assistant director of Learning in Place. He's spent most of his time in front of visitors, working in the Historic Trade Department. Blake also helps manage the "Nightwatchman" tours in the fall, which give visitors a firsthand look at some of the places involved with Old Salem's ghost stories. Blake told me that he himself had an experience a few decades ago in the Single Brothers House that he couldn't explain. He said, "After coming down the stairs, I noticed, clear as day, a coworker head down the hallway and duck into another room. I called out to the individual by name, without receiving a response. I then followed down the hallway to the room and found no one in the location. There were no exits to the room and no one hiding. I to this day can't explain rationally what had taken place, as I know I saw what I believed to be a fellow employee." Despite his experience, Blake insists he's not a believer in the paranormal but would not dismiss anyone claiming to have had an experience.

Blake told me of other employees of Old Salem who have had experiences. A few years ago, one of the VPs was working late in their office at the Single Brothers House. They heard a noise coming from the floor below, as if someone had dragged a heavy piece of furniture. They decided to ignore the noise because "this is an old house and old houses make noises." I can't help but wonder: How often do we see or hear or otherwise experience a spirit but misinterpret it or explain it away as a natural occurrence? Probably about as much as we misinterpret natural occurrences as supernatural. Anyway, Blake said the employee continued to hear strange noises, and they eventually left for the night. After turning on the alarm system, they said out loud, "Okay, I'm leaving now." Later, as they were driving home, they looked up at the electric candles on display in each window for the holiday season and noticed that every candle was lit, except for their office. Upon checking the candle's battery the next day, they found it was in proper working condition. This was a phenomenon that occurred again about a year later. This time, a photograph was taken showing numerous candles turned on, with one conspicuously left off. Some people believe they see the figure of a man standing in that window.

I won't give away all of the wonderful stories that Blake told me—after all, you need to experience some of these stories with fresh eyes upon taking a Nightwatchman tour. But I can't resist telling you about one of my favorite restaurants, Salem Tavern. The original building burned to the ground but was reconstructed in 1784. As you may recall, President Washington himself spent a few nights there in 1791; however, the spirit referred to as the "Tavern Ghost" is perhaps the second-most-well-known guest. Blake told me there have been numerous publications about this ghost, but none of them accurately reflect the "real" story.

It was sometime in the fall of the early 1830s, and it was cold and rainy, when a stranger came knocking at the door very late at night. The man was quite sick, and the tavern keeper managed to get him into a bed. Apparently the stranger was so ill he lost the ability to speak. A local doctor was fetched to see to the stranger, who couldn't even tell his own name. Despite the doctor's best efforts, the strange visitor passed away in the early-morning hours. The man was buried in the "Stranger's Graveyard," a place reserved for non-Moravian burials, but the tavern keeper hadn't lost hope that they might someday identify the deceased stranger, so he stored the man's clothes and personal effects at the tavern.

The legend goes that the departed was so unhappy about being unidentified that over the next few days, the tavern was plagued with "strange noises, cold spots, and the feeling of being followed." Eventually, a maid alerted the tavern keeper that something "spooky" was happening, and he entered the attic, where the stranger's personal belongings had been stored, to investigate. The tavern keeper was astonished to see the shape of the deceased man appear in a cloud of mist. The ghostly spirit apparently gave the tavern keeper some next-of-kin information, which was used to correspond with the man's loved ones. The man was subsequently disinterred and reburied with a proper gravestone, thus putting an end to his haunting at the tavern.

Salem Tavern. Photo by Zack Fox

Great story, right? Well it turns out that it's just that—a story. If you look at the Moravian's own meticulous record, it turns out that the man's identity was known after all. While the real story isn't nearly as fun, it was recorded on September 8, 1831, and reads like this: "Today was the funeral of a gentleman, Samuel McClary, who died night before last in our tavern. He was buried in the Stranger's Graveyard, after an address in English on Luke 12:40 by Br. Reichel. This man came through here on his way to Virginia, seeking a mineral spring there for his failing health. He came here on his return journey, having experienced no benefit, and sought a physician's help; however, he was so weakened and wasted away that nothing could be done for him. One could not ascertain anything about his soul's condition because he was unconscious most of the time."

I asked Blake what he found special about Old Salem, and he told me it was simply the history. He went on: "This is the actual place with buildings on their original foundation. Last year the Single Brothers House celebrated its 250th anniversary. Not too shabby for a building in this country. Not many living-history museums can lay claim to such. As well, we are one of if not the best-documented historical sites in the United States. The Moravians were meticulous record keepers on an institutional level, as most planning, organization, and implementation went through the town's ruling boards. As well, most of the town's residents kept personal diaries that have been preserved. These offer interesting and personal aspects as it related to daily life in the eighteenth and nineteenth centuries. It is said that only 15 percent of the Moravian Archives material has been translated from its Gothic German to English. We'll never know everything as it related to the past, but the more information that you have available, the better the picture that one can paint."

I agree, and what a rich and textured picture can be painted of Old Salem.

PART III

Coastal Tales

CHAPTER 15

The Vampire Beast of Bladenboro

Bladenboro, North Carolina

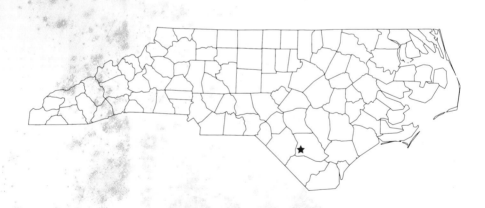

PODCAST • SEASON 3 • EPISODE 1
(September 20, 2019)

Bladenboro, North Carolina, is the very definition of a one-stoplight town. During the 2017 census, Bladenboro reported a population of just 1,657 people. Fifty years ago, it was about half that. But in the early '50s, Bladenboro was overrun by almost 1,000 hunters after a series of bizarre animal attacks put this sleepy little town in the national spotlight.

It began in the waning days of 1953. On December 29, a woman heard her dogs barking and whimpering. She investigated and saw a large, catlike creature running off into the swampy forest that surrounds Bladenboro. That was the first reported sighting of the creature that would become known as the Vampire Beast of Bladenboro.

Over the next week and a half, the police department received report after report of attacks by an animal "like a bear or panther." The creature was described as catlike with very dark fur and somewhere between 3 and 5 feet long.

A creature killed two of Woody Storm's dogs. D. G. Pact saw an animal attack another dog and pull it into the woods. Two of Johnny Vause's dogs were also killed. Then four more were killed. And it wasn't just dogs. Owners also reported that a pet rabbit, some goats, calves, and a couple of hogs had been killed in the same manner as the dogs. Yes, all the victims had died the same way . . . their skulls had been crushed and the body was completely drained of blood.

Then it attacked a human. Mr. and Mrs. Kinslaw heard their dogs baying one night and went out to see what all the ruckus was about. Mrs. Kinslaw said that a large, catlike creature rushed toward her, but her husband scared it away. They said it had a scream "like a woman with a knife stuck in her back." After this, many people were too scared to come out of their houses after dark.

The story was picked up by the newspapers, and nearly 1,000 hunters descended on the small community of barely 900 residents. None of them really knew exactly what they were hunting, though. Speculation included the infamous (and extinct) Carolina panther, the also-extinct eastern Carolina cougar, or perhaps a coyote or a large wolf. The hunters decided that they would rather be safe than sorry, so, in a scene straight out of the movie *Jaws*, they simply went out into the woods and shot anything that moved.

It was a wonder that nobody was killed. Mayor Bob Fussell acknowledged that things had gotten out of control, so he and Police Chief Roy Fores took a large bobcat that had been killed, raised it up the town flagpole, and declared the beast dead.

No one who witnessed the Beast of Bladenboro believed that the bobcat was actually the culprit. The bobcat weighed only 25 pounds, a quarter the size of the beast reported by the witnesses. It was much too small to have killed all those animals.

No further animal attacks were reported, though, and after another week or so, the hunters slowly dissipated and things in Bladenboro returned to normal. Perhaps the hunters had simply made such a racket that they drove the animal far enough into the swampy woods that it was no longer a danger to populated areas.

Even though the Beast of Bladenboro became the best-known mysterious feline of the Carolinas, strange animal attacks had been reported around the state nearly 100 years before the 1954 incident. Most of these attacks were blamed on the infamous Wampus Cat, which you may remember from season 2 of *Carolina Haints*; or a santer, which was sort of the catchall phrase of the time for any mysterious feline.

A story from 1884 may offer some clue as to the creature's origins: When a pair of black tigers escaped from a circus traveling through Virginia, they were last seen headed toward the Great Dismal Swamp, which is split by the Virginia–North Carolina border. Four months later, a Wilmington man believed he killed one of the escaped animals. "It was a fierce-looking brute, even in death; black in color, a male, and measures 6 feet, 6 inches in length, from the end of the nose to the tip of the tail."

A couple of months later, a second black tiger was killed in Sampson County, North Carolina. But the story doesn't end there. A month later, a third black tiger was killed in Greensville County, Virginia. But . . . only two tigers were reported as missing. Could there have been more escaped tigers? In the six months that they were missing, the tigers covered a distance of at least 250 miles. Could they have bred with a native wild cat to produce the Vampire Beast?

A lot of people don't believe that the Beast of Bladenboro ever existed. They believe that the entire thing was a hoax perpetrated by the mayor himself. You see, Mayor Fussell just happened to own the only movie theater in town. And they just happened to be playing a movie titled *The Big Cat* during the crisis. In fact, after hanging the bobcat from the flagpole, the mayor was quoted as saying, "Now you can see the cat! We've got him on our screen! And in Technicolor!"

It was Mayor Fussell who first reported the incidents to the newspapers. Many years later, the mayor described the beast as 10 percent real and 90 percent imagination. He confessed that "a little publicity never hurt a small town."

But just as the legend of the Vampire Beast of Bladenboro was about to go down in the record books as the largest snipe hunt in history . . . the beast returned, this time in the Triad.

Starting in 2004, several North Carolina cities have reported attacks very similar to the Beast of Bladenboro.

In Bolivia, North Carolina, five dogs were killed, including two large, powerful pit bulls. Their heads were crushed and their blood had been drained. One of the 120-pound pit bulls was found in its owner's front yard. The man strapped his pet onto the back of an ATV, drove it out into the woods, and buried it. The man was shocked the following morning to find that "something" had exhumed the pit bull and placed it back in the exact spot where it had been found the previous day.

Other attacks were reported in Charlotte, Lexington, Asheboro, and finally Greensboro, where several of Billy Yow's goats were killed in a manner consistent with the Beast of Bladenboro. Unlike Mayor Bob Fussell, Billy Yow was a credible witness. At the time, he served as the Guilford County commissioner. Before these newer reports subsided, the beast was believed responsible for killing more than fifty animals, some as large as cows and horses.

Is the Beast of Bolivia and the Vampire Beast of Greensboro the same animal that was dubbed as the Beast of Bladenboro? If so, why the fifty-year lull in reported sightings? Were these later attacks a product of the Bladenboro Beast's offspring? Unless one of these animals is killed or captured, we will probably never know.

In 2007, the History Channel show *Monster Quest* ran an episode titled "Vampire Beast," investigating these reports and comparing them to the 1954 Bladenboro attacks. As with most television shows featuring cryptids, the *Monster Quest* team was unable to obtain sufficient evidence to identify the species of beast responsible for the killings. Also, prior to his death, Steve "Crocodile Hunter" Irwin planned to film a show featuring the Vampire Beast of the Carolinas.

A more traditional tale of vampires comes out of Charleston, Tennessee, but this story is no less bizarre or mysterious as the Beast of Bladenboro.

The 1920s saw a huge push across the nation for road improvements to accommodate the growing automobile industry. Bradley County, Tennessee, was no exception. One afternoon while widening the Upper River Road, the crew made a startling discovery. They found the remains of a woman . . . a PETRIFIED woman.

Now, I'm not going to go into the scientific process of petrification, but it typically takes a long time . . . a *really* long time. But the woman appeared to be relatively modern, certainly within the previous fifty years.

Adding to the mystery was the fact that the woman had a wooden stake driven through her heart, which had also petrified.

The adjacent property was owned by the Camp family. Authorities questioned the current Camp family residents, but they claimed to know nothing about it. If their father had ever known who the woman buried on their property was or why she had been treated as a vampire, he never mentioned it to them.

No one else in the neighborhood could even recall there being so much as a RUMOR of vampires. The Appalachian Mountains are full of superstitious tales and legends, some originating from the Native Americans and going back centuries. Yet, nowhere is there any mention of vampires.

The Vampire of Bradley County remains a mystery to this day.

DAN'S STORY

As I sit writing this entry into the book, I can't help but ponder the irony of the situation we're in. I have some formal education in sociology, and the phrase that comes to mind when I think about what happened to Bladenboro in the mid-1950s is "moral panic." It's a peculiar thing, and not something that I would have ever claimed to have lived through myself—until recently. The research team and I had plans to visit the small town of Bladenboro and speak with folks at the historical museum. Unfortunately, those plans have been delayed. The museum is closed for the foreseeable future. And it's not safe to be around groups of people at the moment.

I'm writing this in the early days of spring 2020, and at the moment, schools are closed, businesses are closed, and concerts and sporting events are canceled. The World Health Organization has declared the outbreak of COVID-19, also known as the coronavirus, as a global pandemic. National, state, and local governments are planning for worst-case scenarios and trying to keep the economy from slipping into a nearly inevitable recession. Folks are walking around in public—that's the ones brave enough, or stupid enough—with gloves and surgical masks protecting their faces. Drive-up testing stations have been erected at area hospitals. Meats, bottled water, and toilet paper are almost impossible to find in the stores.

A few weeks ago, I would have said that it would be difficult to imagine what it's like living through a moral panic, the likes of which were brought on by the infamous "Beast" in Bladenboro. But as I sit to write this passage, still having not visited Bladenboro, as was planned, I think I'm starting to understand the type of fear and anxiety that folks may have experienced. No, this isn't quite the same. For one, the small town of fewer than 1,000 residents was under siege by a bevy of hunters, journalists, and just interested parties. This once-unknown town was the talk of the country for a short while, and then it just went away. While I hope and pray that the current predicament we find ourselves in happens to resolve itself in a similar fashion, the truth is that no one knows what will happen next. Perhaps that's the root of a moral panic itself, the common denominator of uncertainty.

As a consolation for missing out on visiting Bladen County, I was able to speak with Henry Singletary of the Bladenboro Historical Society Museum. Singletary was seven years old when the "Beast" struck his hometown, but he remembers it well: "It was some kind of animal that killed some livestock and some pets. It got people pretty scared around here. Parents were not letting their children out of the house in some cases. Nobody knew exactly what the animal was, and still don't, for that matter. It lasted for a couple weeks; it started in December and by about the second week of January there was nothing happening. There were a lot of people who didn't go out at night because they just didn't know what this thing was."

Singletary remembers "a couple of people over at the cotton mill village where a couple of pets were killed in their yard—their fear was enhanced by some teenage boys who went around making animal noises and shaking the bushes. I've known a couple of people slightly older than me who told me they did that. But regarding the animal that killed other animals, something actually did that."

I was curious to know how life changed in the area during that time. Singletary lived a little ways out of town limits and doesn't remember having to abide by a curfew, but he recalled that "within a few months after it happened, everything went back to normal. Living out in the country, after a few months, it was no problem for us children to go out in the woods—probably the most dangerous part was we had all these hunters come in from everywhere. It's kind of a wonder that somebody didn't shoot somebody; *that* danger was real. For those few weeks it was not uncommon to see trucks going up and down the road with dogs and hunters and guns sticking out every which way. They were hunting for something, but no one could identify exactly what it was."

Perhaps the most fascinating thing about this whole ordeal to me is the lasting impact it's had on the community. You might half expect it to be a dirty little secret that folks aren't willing to talk about, but you'd be wrong. I asked Singletary how the story gained popularity over the years and became such an integral part of the town's social fabric. He said, "The folklore stories continued to circle around, of course. With the internet, if one person gets interested and starts inquiring, it causes a storm of other inquiries. It kind of went away, but because of the people who remembered it, a few years ago the town was looking for a way to have a festival." This led to the creation of the annual Beast Fest.

In Bladenboro, the "Beast" is wholeheartedly embraced, and hell . . . it's even celebrated! I think maybe I'll save my trip to Bladenboro for the annual Beast Fest, hosted by Boost the 'Boro, Inc., a nonprofit group designed to promote tourism and cultural enrichment in the community. At the annual Beast Fest, there's a "Beast" mascot roaming the grounds, and there's live music, dancing in the streets, food vendors, craftsmen, storytelling, and a community experience that can't be found anywhere else.

Given our modern-day boogeyman, Singletary said it was too early to tell about Beast Fest this year, but he's hopeful, since all "money raised is for doing things to make it a little bit better town. It's intended to draw attention to the town" and has been "very successful, and every year has been bigger and bigger. There's live entertainment—bigger names and local talent—of course they have about every kind of vendor you can imagine. Bladenboro has been in decline over the past few years with our industry leaving, and so as far as in the town limits, there might only be a couple of thousand people. This last Beast Fest, I think it was said there was something like 40,000 people. That's drawing in people pretty good!"

I myself cannot wait to make it to Bladenboro for the next Beast Fest, whenever that may be. I want to get a T-shirt, speak to some local natives about their stories, listen to some soul, and eat me a collard green sandwich with a thick slice of fatback. "You've got to come down here and eat one of those," Singletary tells me. He also said there's not that many people left who remember those few fateful weeks. I'd love to get down there and meet some of them while I can. I just hope that our current moral panic—the one shared by my town and Bladenboro, and all over the world—hasn't put an end to this awesome festival.

CHAPTER 16

Joe Baldwin and the Maco Light

Maco, North Carolina

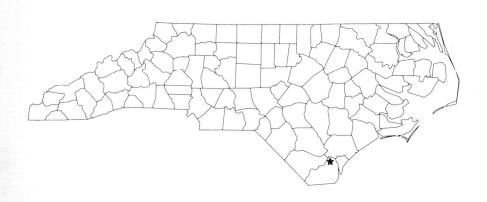

PODCAST • SEASON 2 • EPISODE 5
(November 2, 2018)

Grover Cleveland was the twenty-second president of the United States. He served in office in the late 1800s, before the widespread production of the automobile. So, like those who served before him, he relied on the rail service when traveling the country.

Cleveland's train pulled into Maco Station on an unusually warm February night in 1889. His days in office were numbered, and he knew that this was most likely his last train ride as president. He was a lame-duck president. He had lost the reelection campaign to that Republican clout, Benjamin Harrison, and in just two weeks' time, he would be out of office.

So nobody could blame him if he arrived at the station in a foul mood. But, on the contrary, he was in fine spirits. He took a stroll along the tracks and was quite courteous to the folks that he met, talking with each one at length before moving on.

It was at this point that he noticed the signalman using two lanterns: a red one and a green one. He knew that the traditional train signal was a single white light. So he asked the man about it. The story began thirty years prior, in the spring of 1867, a few miles outside Wilmington. A light, misting rain fed the fog that hung thick in the air. A lonely country road hugged the Wilmington–Manchester railroad track, and together they cut a path through the eastern North Carolina swamps and pines to their destination: the depot in the small community of Maco, North Carolina.

Joe Baldwin was in the caboose as the train neared Maco Station. Suddenly the car lurched and began to lose speed. He rushed to the front of the car, opening the door to see the train receding in the distance. Under normal circumstances it wouldn't be that big of a deal. But at night with the fog and rain, it was a different story. Joe knew that another train would be coming up track in just a few minutes. In these weather conditions, the second train wouldn't be able to see the disabled caboose. For a second, Joe considered just running away. Who could blame him? But the second train was a passenger train. If he abandoned his post, Joe thought, how many people would be hurt . . . or worse, killed? He had to try to warn them.

He snatched the lantern from its post and went out onto the small ledge at the back of the car. He heard the passenger train drawing near, and he began frantically waving the lantern to signal the conductor. It almost worked.

The engineer of the passenger train saw Joe's signal and slammed on the brakes. The screeching whine of metal on metal echoed through the darkness as the train fought to arrest its momentum, but in the end, Joe was too late. The second train was not able to stop in time. As Joe's train car crept over the trestle of Rattlesnake Creek, the passenger train slammed into it, killing him and, some say, severing his head from his body.

A head that was lost in the swamp and never found.

Or so the legend goes . . .

It wasn't very long after the terrible accident that claimed Joe's life when people started reporting seeing a strange light along the tracks at night.

Oddly, it almost always followed the same path. It would appear about a mile outside Maco Station, near the Rattlesnake Creek trestle. It was dim at first, moving slowly, but as it went along it would grow brighter and faster. Occasionally it would zigzag back and forth as it moved forward. It moved like a man swinging a lantern. It never strayed more than a few feet from the tracks. More often than not, once it reached a certain point on the rails, it reversed itself, eventually ending up in the exact place it had started from. Then it was said to fade from view, often to reappear only half an hour later and repeat the same cycle.

Locals said it was the ghost of Old Joe Baldwin, searching for his lost head.

The light would manifest itself regularly, especially in the early 1900s. It was rare for a calendar month to pass without the light making an appearance, sometimes showing itself several nights in a row.

A lot has changed in the 150 years since Joe's fateful accident. At that time, the area was known as Rattlesnake Grade, a sleepy little spot in the northern tip of Brunswick County. Eventually, because of Joe Baldwin's fateful accident, Rattlesnake Grade came to be known as Maco. In 1977 the railroad tracks were removed and the trestle over Rattlesnake Creek was dismantled. Unfortunately, since then the sightings of the Maco Light have all but stopped.

Before the tracks were removed, the Maco Light could manifest at any time; it seemed to appear most often during the summer months. In fact, the phenomenon happened with such regularity that it soon began to disrupt rail service. Engineers would often misinterpret the light as a warning signal and stop their train on the tracks. For safety reasons, the railroad company ordered that the standard white warning light be discontinued in the vicinity of Maco Station. Instead, they were told to use two lights . . . yep, you guessed it: a red one and a green one, just like President Cleveland witnessed.

It's thought that the president did not see the Maco Light for himself, but he was intrigued nonetheless. He shared Joe Baldwin's tale when he returned to Washington, and suddenly the Maco Lights garnered national attention, leading to an increase of tourism to the tiny burg. Psychics, professors, investigators, and scores upon scores of curious onlookers made the journey south. Over the years, thousands of people have visited the area in hopes of witnessing the spectacle for themselves.

By the 1950s and '60s, in the midst of all this exposure, the Maco Light peaked in popularity, when dozens of people would park on the road beside the track each night and watch for the light to make an appearance. Many people came to Maco in order to explain away the mystery. Even the Smithsonian

Institution investigated the phenomenon after President Cleveland brought it to their attention.

Over the years, many theories have been presented to explain the Maco Lights . . . many of them sound just like the theories presented to explain the Brown Mountain Lights in Linville, and just like those theories, none of them hold up to rational analysis. As you would expect, some people chalked up the light to swamp gas or St. Elmo's fire or the reflection of car headlights from the nearby highway. Even though the lights were reported far before the automobile came to rural eastern North Carolina, and St. Elmo's fire happens only during electrically charged thunderstorms, whereas the Maco Light could be seen at any time. Anyone who has seen swamp gas would know that it would not confine itself to staying only above the tracks. Swamp gas would naturally drift throughout the swampy woodland without direction or cause.

Eventually the United States Army got involved. A machine gun detachment was sent from Fort Bragg under orders to either discover the source of the mystery or blast it into oblivion; however, the light did not show itself while the army was in town.

One interesting theory involves a fault line that hypothetically runs beneath the tracks. Although no fault line has ever been found, earthquakes have been felt in Wilmington, Charleston, and Savannah. Maco lies at the northern end of the proposed line. The theory speculates that the Maco Light was caused by static electricity produced by the pressures imposed by the fault line. The static charge would use the steel train tracks as a conductor and discharge as light along their path. This theory explains why the light has not been seen since the tracks were removed.

Of course, various psychics and ghost hunters have maintained that the light is Joe Baldwin, who is unaware that he has passed away, vehemently trying to warn oncoming trains.

Similar "headless conductor" stories have been associated to other alleged ghost lights around the country . . . the Bragg Road Light in Southeast Texas, the Paulding Light in Michigan's Upper Peninsula, and the Gurdon Light of Arkansas, which, ironically, also runs atop the New Madrid fault line. However, the Maco Light manifested many years before any of the others and, some say, is the inspiration for the other stories.

Many magazine and newspaper articles have been written about the phenomenon. The *Wilmington Star-News* covered the light several times over the years. Even *Life* magazine ran an article in 1957, in an era when the magazine was at the height of its popularity.

A man named James Burke researched the records in the Wilmington Railroad Museum. He found no records to indicate that anyone named Joe Baldwin had been killed on the tracks; however, another story was found, remarkably similar to the legend. A conductor named Charles Baldwin took his train to retrieve a car that had become decoupled and was stranded on the tracks. Misjudging his speed, Baldwin slammed into the helpless car. Although Charles was not decapitated in the accident, he died a few days later from injuries sustained in the accident. The accident report laid the blame on Charles for failing to hang a lantern on the train as required.

DAN'S STORY

The Maco Light is one of the most frustrating stories we've covered on *Carolina Haints*. The story itself is so old, there's no one to talk to who remembers anything. The best I could hope for there is someone who potentially remembers the tracks before they were pulled up in 1977. That's supposedly when the ghostly sight of Joe Baldwin's glowing lantern was last seen.

From researching the area itself, I feel like it's such a tease. From first glance at a map, it appears that Maco doesn't even exist anymore, but if you look close enough, it's there, west of Leland along Highway 74. The elusive Wilmington & Manchester Railroad was said to have derailed near the curvy spot in the tracks known as Rattlesnake Grade, near Hood Creek.

From a map, you can see Hood Creek running roughly north and south and crossing under I-74/76. If anything, Maco appears to be an unincorporated community in what has been officially designated Sandy Creek. Why officially? Because it's an incorporated town with a town hall on Sandy Creek Drive. Okay, it's a double-wide trailer, but it's still a government building.

And what tiny street should happen to sit cozily in between two other streets, just blocks from the town hall? Why, that would be Joe Baldwin Drive. There's also

Maco Road, which runs from Highway 17 near the community of Winnabow to Highway 74 in Sandy Creek. Near the Hardee's and Dollar General, what small street should Maco Road intersect with? That would be *Old* Maco Road, which is just around the corner from the gas station . . . Maco Depot.

Everywhere I look, there are clues to connections with this story. It's infuriating! While I couldn't find Rattlesnake Creek anywhere in proximity, just 30 miles north in Pender County is a small creek, barely visible on a map and practically in the middle of nowhere, near the unincorporated community of Ivanhoe, with the name Big Rattlesnake Creek.

Sandy Creek was incorporated in 1988 and is so close to the town of Leland that they share the same zip code. According to the town's own website, the physical address of their own town hall is actually in Leland. A decade ago, Sandy Creek had a population of just 318 people. According to Brunswick County's Wikipedia page, Maco is one of twenty-eight unincorporated communities in the county, along with twenty-five towns such as Bolivia, Shallote, and Holden Beach.

I spoke with the town clerk, Marion Evans, who confirmed for me that Joe Baldwin Drive is in fact named after the folklore. Evans went on to say, "The oldest local residents believe this area is where the train wreck occurred along the portions of railroad tracks that once ran through this area, now known as Sandy Creek." What a great example of oral history and storytelling. Even the oldest residents of Sandy Creek wouldn't be old enough to remember the disaster, but their grandparents or great-grandparents might.

This is the very basis of folklore and tradition—someone's Granny tells them of the time she saw old Joe Baldwin's lantern swinging back and forth at this very

spot. That grandchild then tells their son the story, perhaps losing some of the panache or flavor, or who knows, the story could pick up steam (pun intended) and be full of embellishments. In this particular case, an elderly resident was told by someone who remembers, or perhaps who has seen the ghostly light themselves, then passed it along to the town clerk, who passed it to me. Now, I humbly relay to you, the closest thing you can get to visiting and being a part of this story is taking a turn off I-74 and traveling a few blocks south to the little residential street of Joe Baldwin Drive.

I asked if the tiny town of Sandy Creek has ever done anything to promote tourism by using the story. Evans told me they had not. Perhaps they could embrace the tale and make a festival out of it like nearby Bladenboro did with its famous Beast Fest. Or maybe they could hire a local storyteller to host a lantern-lit story night for kids. I can't think of a better way to keep the tradition alive for future generations.

A few weeks before this book's deadline was due, Jeffrey Cochran and I took a day trip to Sandy Creek to look at Joe Baldwin Drive in person. While there, we got a chance to meet Marion in person, and she was able to point out for us the actual placement of the old train tracks. She told us to head back out toward Highway 74 and to look for an elevated impression just south of the roadway. According to Marion, the long strip of land where the tracks used to lie can be seen there, but what's more difficult to see is how it backs up to the houses that run along Joe Baldwin Drive.

Jeff and I made our way back to the entrance to the small community. We got out of the car and walked along the side of the road. It wasn't immediately apparent to us where the tracks were. As I walked along a small bump in the ground, likely put in place for irrigation purposes, Jeff walked up a hill and then turned to me to say, "Here it is." I hastily made my way to him, and damn if he wasn't right. You could clearly see what Marion was talking about; it was a long, straight path through the woods, clear of brush and trees. The stretch of land was noticeably elevated and sat approximately 50 to 100 feet south of the highway. We walked along it as far as we could without trespassing on private property.

While walking along the path of what used to be the Wilmington & Manchester Railroad line, I was overcome with the desire for a metal detector to look for railroad spikes. I couldn't think of a better souvenir than an old, rusty, twisted hunk of metal, except for maybe a spooky old lantern. I eventually recalled my folklore, and it occurred to me that it's an incredibly bad idea to take something away from a haunted site. Many people have taken pieces of brick or stone from various places infamous for their haunted legends, only to bring their souvenirs back in a desperate attempt to make their own haunting stop. I have enough problems to worry about. I'll stick to taking pictures.

CHAPTER 17

The Flaming Ship of Ocracoke

Ocracoke Island, North Carolina

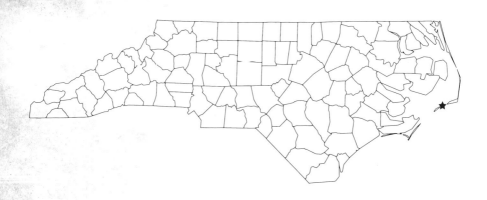

PODCAST • SEASON 1 • EPISODE 13
(February 23, 2018)

The Diamond Shoals are located just off Ocracoke Island, between Ocracoke Inlet and Cape Hatteras. These waters have long been known by sailors to be . . . unusual. As part of the Graveyard of the Atlantic, this area has racked up more than 600 shipwrecks. Science tells us that it is the weather that makes these waters so unpredictable. Two powerful ocean currents converge at this point—the Gulf Stream from the south and the Labrador Current from the north. They swirl and churn the seabed into the ever-changing labyrinth of the Diamond Shoals. This, combined with the fact that more hurricanes have passed through these waters than in any other point of the North Atlantic, makes this one of the most dangerous places in the world for maritime navigation.

But the weather isn't to blame for *all* of the shipwrecks off the North Carolina coast. The cruelty and greed of the deviant human nature led to countless deaths in these waters. These were among some of the favorite territories for pirates in the 1700s. Blackbeard himself kept a house in Bath, North Carolina, right next door to Governor Edward Hyde.

One such tale is shrouded in legend and speculation, as many of these tales are, but one thing *is* for sure: it all started with a little-known war in the picturesque Rhine region of what is now Germany. The Palatinate War was a struggle between Louis XIV of France and William III of England from 1688 to 1697. The war was known by several names, including the Nine Years War and the War of the Grand Alliance. France and Spain had been slowly advancing into neighboring territories, causing the rest of central Europe to get rather . . . nervous. They began to fear that the partnership between France and Spain would lead to an empire.

Several countries came together to form their own version of the United Nations, a coalition of power between England and the German states. Today this would be the territories of England, Ireland, Scotland, Germany, Poland, Belgium, Luxemburg, the Czech Republic, Slovakia, Austria, Croatia, the Netherlands, Portugal, and Sweden. They called it the League of Augsburg, or the Grand Alliance.

In 1688, the inevitable happened when France invaded the Palatinate, the area around Cologne (Köln), Germany. The Grand Alliance responded to France's advancements and in 1689 drove them back in retreat. As France withdrew from the Rhine valley, they burned every town, village, and castle they came to. The Nine Years War, as the name implies, would not be over until 1697.

France's razing of the German countryside displaced about 10,000 people. Most of them found their way to England for refuge. These were not beggars; they were skilled workers, and the ramifications of such a vast influx of workers threatened to cripple England's economy. A Swiss baron,

Christophe Von Graffenried, proposed a solution. He took a total of 2,000 refugees to the province of the Carolinas. First, he took shiploads of refugees from his own country to the New World. They established the city of New Bern (named after Bern, the capital of Switzerland). New Bern became the second town established in the province and later became the home of the first state capital. Then they arranged for some of the Palatinate refugees to join them. Not all of them made it.

As I said, these refugees were not poor. They paid for their passage across the Atlantic with gold, silver, coins, and jewels that they had kept hidden as they fled Germany. During the passage to America, their valuables were hidden in the trunks they kept close to them in the sleeping quarters. They dressed as meagerly as they could while on the ship.

Ocracoke Inlet was the point of entry for ships in those days. Most ships did not risk navigating the treacherous waters any farther than that. It was customary to deposit their passengers and cargo in Pilot Town (today's Ocracoke Village), then smaller vessels could take them to their final destination without fear of grounding on the shallow shoals.

The passengers, especially the children, were full of excitement. After weeks at sea, they could see the lights of Pilot Town and smell the wood fires that cooked their morning meals. They had made it safely to the New World.

The captain told them that he would take all the passengers into Pilot Town, but it wasn't efficient for him to take all their stuff. He said that they would load their trunks directly on the smaller boats when they came. The Palatines went below deck to get ready. Feeling like they were finally safe, they took off the rags they were wearing and put on their finest outfits. Not wanting to leave all of their valuables behind, they emerged back on deck in their fine clothes, carrying all their gold and jewels.

It was more gold than the captain and crew had ever seen. What the Germans did not know was that the captain had once been a pirate. He had accepted the "King's pardon" and swore to lead a law-abiding life. And so far, he had. But this was a temptation too great to pass up. He quickly gathered the crew and told them what he had in mind. They were all with him.

The captain told his passengers that there was a problem with the small boats. They would have to wait until the next morning to go into town. He suggested that they go back below deck and get some rest. The Palatines had no reason not to believe him. They took their belongings and returned to their quarters.

That night was the first new moon of the month of September. Late that night, there were a few Germans catching some night air up on deck; the rest of the Palatines were fast asleep. The captain led the crew silently throughout the ship. First, they strangled those above deck with lengths of rope. Then they went below deck and quickly cut the throats of everyone on board. Men. Women. Children. They spared no one.

The crew searched all the trunks and chests and deposited the valuables they found on the deck of the ship. They divided the booty evenly among them. Before abandoning the ship on the same longboats that *would* have carried the Palatines to safety, they cut the ship's anchor, doused the decks in oil, and set the vessel on fire.

They knew that the prevailing winds would push the ship to the northeast, so they rowed due west. They laughed loudly, pleased with their bounty regardless of the loss of life that it took to obtain it. Then one of the men looked behind them.

Instead of drifting slowly to the northeast as it should have been, the ship was barreling straight toward them at full speed! It was fully engulfed in flames, but that didn't seem to slow it down any. The men started rowing; rowing with everything they had. Rowing in vain.

As the huge ship crushed their longboat, they could hear long, mournful wails coming from the ship, like the sound of a thousand tormented souls all crying out as one.

Most of the men drowned, but a few were able to cling to the debris and make it to shore. The treasure sank to the bottom of Pamlico Sound, and then, although no one was at the helm, the ship turned back to the northeast and sailed out of sight.

It is said that to this day, with the first new moon of September, the flaming ship reappears off the coast of Ocracoke Island. Those who have seen it say that you can smell the acrid odors of the burning ship: canvas, tar, and hemp. And that regardless of the direction of the wind, the ship *always* sails to the northeast.

Not a single piece of the Palatine treasure has ever been found.

DAN'S STORY

I recently took a trip to Ocracoke Island. It's a beautiful spot where you can go and truly feel disconnected from the mainland. Tourism, gift shops, and cafes with pirate themes can be found all around the village. I found it to be a quaint, almost magical place—a place where the very air you breathe is filled with the history and mystery of pirates and their hidden treasures.

You can still find a few folks who speak "Hoi Toid," a disappearing dialect of native O'cockers, also known as "the Ocracoke brogue." It's a byproduct of isolation in which some of the pronunciation and the words themselves are a holdover and mutate over time, from Old English. It's one of the things that make this place so special. You can't go to Charlotte or Fayetteville and expect to hear anything close to Hoi Toid. To give you some sort of idea as to what it sounds like, the words "hoi toid" themselves mean "high tide." This brief translation should give you some idea of what it sounds like, but that doesn't mean you're likely to keep up with a conversation among native islanders. They might refer to you as a "dingbatter," a playful term for nonislanders.

To get to the island, my wife and I took a forty-five-minute ferry ride from Cape Hatteras. Our legs were still tired from having marched to the top of the iconic lighthouse. We were also able to visit the graveyard of the Atlantic Museum to look at some recovered wreckage. So when we finally got to sit still and breathe the sea air, we quite enjoyed our brief boat ride and used the opportunity to relax before continuing on our journey through the outer banks. Upon arriving at the island, it seemed pretty wild and unmanned. The island itself is about 15 miles long, and you have to drive a few miles south to get to the village.

Perhaps my favorite thing to see on the trip was the lighthouse. A relatively short and solid white structure, Ocracoke's is the oldest working lighthouse on the East Coast. We ate some great seafood at Howard's Pub and followed it up with some souvenir shopping at Teach's Hole, a Blackbeard-themed gift shop. One legend says that Ocracoke got its name from Blackbeard's eager shouting for the cock to crow so that he may commence battle at the first light of day. At Springer's Point, on the sound side of the island, it's said that the pirate met his demise. Try as I might, it's difficult to describe Ocracoke, but it's simply a magical place. Believe me, I'm so looking forward to returning for a longer stay. I'm counting the days. If you're looking for a calm, isolated place to visit that's steeped in history and haunts, I can't think of a much-better place.

A native islander might read my entry in this chapter and realize it's a bit *whopperjawed* (yes, I could write that more plainly but I'm not going to). I've been to the island only once, I'm sad to say. This makes me a far cry from an expert on the subject, so I decided to speak with an expert—Mr. Philip Howard. Although he wasn't born or raised on Ocracoke, he's an eighth-generation native and has lived there for fifty years. He owns and operates the Village Craftsmen, a local store that sells crafts and hosts walking ghost tours. According to Howard, "I started it in 1970 in a teepee and then I built the building it's currently housed in in 1973. I've added on to it a little bit since, but it's still a small family-run business. It's right across the street from our family cemetery, where my parents, my grandparents, my great-grandparents, my great-great-grandparents, and my great-great-great-grandparents are buried."

In addition to this, he's also written two books about Ocracoke ghost stories, both of which have been very successful and are in numerous printings. The first one is called *Digging Up Uncle Evans,* and the second is *Howard Street Hauntings.*

Howard told me of his company's walking ghost tours: "I started the ghost tours about fifteen years ago now; we do Tuesdays and Fridays, just in the summer. Oh my God, they're really popular. We try to limit the numbers to like two dozen at a time, but we sometimes take thirty or more, and we still have to turn people away. I don't want it to get too big because then people can't hear well. But people love them! And we never do that business about promoting the idea that ghosts really exist. We use them as an opportunity to share island history with people, and they love that. We don't dress up in costumes or hire someone to jump out and scare people, but we tell the stories as we've heard them."

As you might've imagined, I'm a big fan of North Carolina folklore books. Between Jeff Cochran and me, we have dozens of books that we use as resources. If pressed to say who my favorite of those authors might be, I'd have to say Charles Harry Whedbee, who wrote *Legends of the Outer Banks and Tar Heel Tidewater*, among several notable others. One of my personal favorites is his first-person recounting of a visit to Ocracoke in his teens in which he tells the tale of "Blackbeard's Cup." In the story, Whedbee describes a mysterious visit he made with a friend to a small building in which his friend uttered the secret password, "Death to Spottiswood," and was granted entry into a meeting of a secret society of native islanders who all spoke Hoi Toid. I won't spoil the reveal for you, but let's just say it's in the title.

Howard told me he's also a fan, but admitted, "I'll be perfectly honest with you; I'm not sure whether you want to hear this or not. Charles Whedbee was a great writer and a wonderful storyteller. His first book is comprised of authentic legends of the Outer Banks that were collected from people from Nags Head all the way down to Ocracoke. But they were so popular and he was such a good writer that these other books came out and . . . nobody on Ocracoke had ever heard of the Flaming Ship of Ocracoke until that book came out."

Howard went on to say that "the Blackbeard's Cup business—I didn't grow up on Ocracoke, but my father was born and raised here, and we came to Ocracoke every year as I was growing up. And I've lived here for fifty years now. My family goes back to William Howard, who bought Ocracoke in 1759; he bought the whole island. So I have a long history here, although I wasn't born and raised here. But that story of the Blackbeard's Cup is just so foreign to Ocracoke people. It was written by somebody who obviously knew something about, if not was in, a college fraternity or some other secret organization. Now there is a Masonic lodge on Ocracoke, and there's been one here for quite a long time. But as far as a secret society, that's a totally made-up story. It's a great story! I love it! Same with the Flaming Ship. They're both great stories. He's a good storyteller. Who knows, the stories in *Legends of the Outer Banks* may have been made up too, but at least they were passed down from generation to generation; they weren't written just to sell some books. So I wouldn't put much faith in any of those stories past the first book, *Legends of the Outer Banks*, as being historically accurate. That's not to say, accurate as far as what really happened, because all ghost stories are just stories."

Howard told me the story of the Stovepipe Hat shipwreck from the mid-1860s, in which a ship was loaded with stovepipe hats, and after it wrecked, "they were all washed ashore on Hatteras Island, and that Easter everybody was wearing stovepipe hats around the village. It was a great story, and I wanted to know more about it so I started doing some research, and I finally discovered that the whole thing was made up. It wasn't a real story at all."

Howard reminded me that despite the true history behind these legends, truth is subjective and the value in a great tale of folklore is often in the story itself and its telling. Knowing the true story behind the lore doesn't have to diminish the story itself. You can almost look at it like a film adaptation from a novel. The film is merely a reimagining of something that already exists; it doesn't damage or necessarily tarnish the original narrative. Hell, sometimes it can even improve on it; there are plenty of classic films that are better than the works they're based on (I'm looking at you, *Jaws* and *Forrest Gump*).

In an article he wrote for the magazine *Skeptical Enquirer,* Howard quotes author Mary Roach from her book *Spook,* in which she said, "Debunkers are probably right, but they're no fun to visit a graveyard with." Howard admits that he's a bit of a skeptic but, like me, enjoys the stories themselves for the story's sake. After all, for many, the stories are a pathway into learning about a place's history. Howard told me he always ends his ghost tours by telling his guests how much he appreciates them for participating, because "Ocracoke is not just land. This is not a fake community; this is a real community, and we really enjoy being able to share some of our stories and some of our history."

I don't know about you, but I for one thoroughly enjoy them.

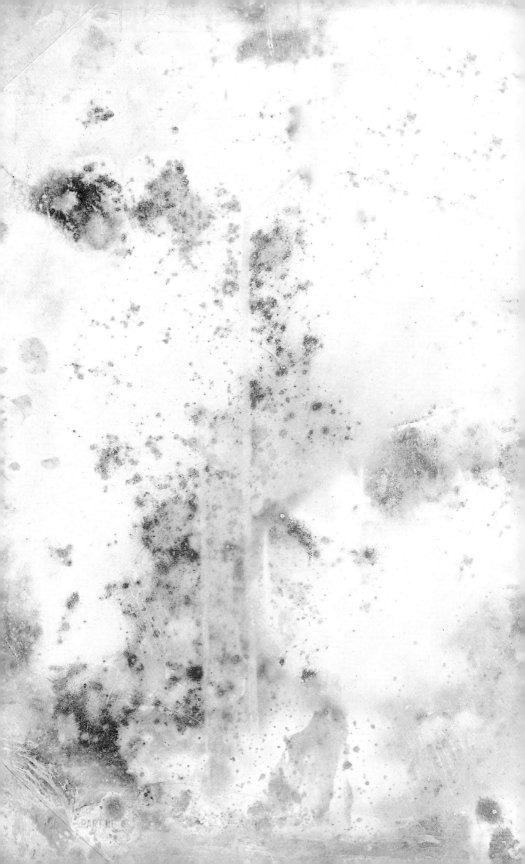

CHAPTER 18

The Mysterious Disappearance of Theodosia Burr

Nags Head, North Carolina

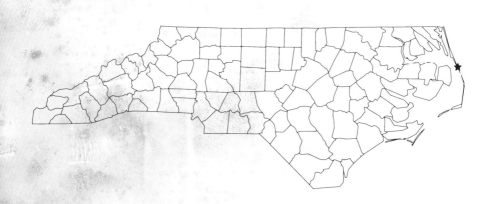

PODCAST • SEASON 1 • EPISODE 10
(January 22, 2018)

Theodosia Burr Alston was born into a life of privilege. Her father was Aaron Burr, vice president to Thomas Jefferson. Her mother, Theodosia Bartow Prevost Burr, was a key supporter of the American Revolution, and she married Joseph Alston, the governor of South Carolina. So, of course, Theodosia Burr Alston was wont for nothing, right? Well, as we all know, life always seems to find a way to throw a curveball.

There is nothing particularly spooky about the first part of Theodosia's story, but, bear with us—it's an interesting portrayal of American history. Theodosia Bartow Prevost offered her family home, the Hermitage, in Ho-Ho-Kus, New Jersey, to be used as a meeting place for patriots during the American Revolution. Among the regular visitors to the estates were Alexander Hamilton, the Marquis de Lafayette, William Livingston, and Jeremiah Wadsworth. During the Battle of Monmouth, George Washington stayed at the Hermitage.

During this time, she met her future husband, Aaron Burr. At the time, she was still married to Jacques Marcus Prevost, whose health was ailing. In 1781, Jacques Prevost passed away, and Theodosia married Aaron Burr a few months later. Theodosia Bartow Prevost Burr bore a daughter in 1783 and named the infant after herself. The elder Theodosia was a huge influence on young Theodosia Burr's life, but she succumbed to stomach cancer when Theodosia was just eleven years old.

Aaron Burr was a highly decorated soldier during the Revolutionary War, rising to the rank of colonel before having to resign for health reasons. After leaving the front lines of the war, Burr continued to support the Revolution in whatever way he could. Meanwhile, he studied in New York and became a lawyer. This led him into the world of politics. Over the next few years, he served as the New York attorney general and then was elected to the United States Senate in 1791. In 1796, he ran for president of the United States but lost to John Adams.

Burr hatched a plan for the election of 1800. He worked with Thomas Jefferson, helping secure votes for Jefferson in exchange for Burr serving as vice president. This time, his plan succeeded and Aaron Burr became the vice president to the third president of the United States; however, Jefferson didn't really trust or like Burr and dropped him from the ticket for the 1804 election.

Both of her parents were adamant that Theodosia Burr received as much, or more, of an education as any wealthy *male* child would. She absorbed all the training that her father's tutors could give her. She worshiped her father and wanted nothing more than to delight him with her progress— and delight him she did. She was tutored in a wide variety of subjects: the classics, arithmetic, language, music, dance, and even horsemanship. By the age of three she could read and write, and before the age of ten she had read the 4,000-page *Decline and Fall of the Roman Empire*. Theodosia's father never let her education falter despite his own lofty political aspirations.

She studied a variety of languages—Greek, Latin, French—alongside English composition. During the course of her life, Theodosia practiced her composition by writing *thousands* of letters to her father, and he responded to every single one. He also corrected and critiqued them. At an early age, she became widely known for her academic accomplishments.

Aaron Burr and Alexander Hamilton were once close friends; often their families would dine together. But over the years, their relationship began to sour. They often found themselves on opposing sides of the political arena, and when Burr won his seat as senator from New York, he did so by defeating Hamilton's father-in-law.

In 1799, Burr founded the Bank of Manhattan Company, but he did so by telling investors—including Alexander Hamilton—that he was raising capital to construct a water treatment plant for the city of New York. At the eleventh hour, after the funds had been secured, Burr changed the charter of the company to include the financial institution. Hamilton and the others felt duped. Moreover, Burr's duplicity set back the water plant's construction by years, all in a time when malaria tore through the streets of New York because they lacked a source of safe drinking water.

So when Burr found out that Jefferson was going to betray him in the 1804 election, he immediately ran for governor of New York. Alexander Hamilton supported the opposition's campaign, saying that Burr was "a dangerous man and one who ought not be trusted with the reins of government." Burr lost the campaign and never forgave Hamilton for what he called slanderous remarks. He demanded Hamilton retract his statement, but the man refused.

Their feud culminated in Aaron Burr challenging Alexander Hamilton to a duel. Dueling was illegal in the state of New York and carried the death penalty. It was also against the law in New Jersey, but the penalties were less severe, so the men agreed to meet just outside Weehawken, New Jersey, on the morning of July 11, 1804.

From here on, the accounts vary on the actions and intents of the duelists. Many claim that Hamilton had talked for days about the fact that he intended to miss Burr on purpose; however, on the morning of the duel, Hamilton swayed the advantage in his favor. He provided the guns that would be used during the event and, having intimate familiarity with the weapons, had adjusted the trigger on his pistol to have a hair trigger—requiring just half a pound of pressure to fire the bullet—while Burr's weapon was set at its maximum, 10-pound trigger. For comparison, most modern pistols come stock with a 5-to-6-pound trigger pull.

As a result, Hamilton fired first. Whether it was his intention or not, he missed Burr; however, Burr's shot struck Hamilton just above the right hip, causing internal damage to his liver and spine. Alexander Hamilton died the following day. Aaron Burr was brought up on multiple charges in both New York and New Jersey; however, all charges were later dropped, and he never stood trial in either state.

Following the Hamilton incident, Burr devised a new plan to gain the power and glory he had always chased after—and also to alleviate the massive debts that his political aspirations had cost him. He moved to part of Louisiana with more than eighty men and began training them in advanced military tactics. He sensed that there would soon be a war with Spain over the Mexican territories, and when it happened, he planned on seizing the lands in the Southwest of the United States for himself. The land from what is now Texas to California was under Mexican control; however, during an uprising, it would be up for grabs. He planned to make himself king of this new territory, but the Adam-Onis Treaty secured Florida for the United States without conflict, and war in Texas did not break out until 1836, the year Burr died.

In 1807, Burr had a falling-out with one of his generals, James Wilkinson. The general found his revenge by betraying Burr's plans to President Jefferson, who then declared Burr a traitor and ordered him arrested. Burr was arrested five times as a traitor, but he was never convicted. Despite Jefferson's demands that Burr should be hanged for treason, what Burr had planned to do was only a misdemeanor at that time, and no evidence was ever presented to a grand jury that he had committed treason.

Even though Burr was found innocent, his creditors still hounded him for his political debts. He ended up fleeing to England for several years before returning to New York and living out his days in relative obscurity.

While the Burr family was quite well to do, Theodosia's mother was really the affluent one in the relationship. Aaron Burr's political aspirations came at a pretty large financial cost. Following his wife's death, Burr often found himself fretting over money matters. Since he and his daughter were so close, this was a burden he shared with her.

In 1801, Theodosia found a solution that she thought might alleviate some of her father's woes; she married Joseph Alston. They were the first couple ever on record as having honeymooned at Niagara Falls, New York.

Joseph Alston was born to a very wealthy family in All Saints Parish, South Carolina. He was in the law program at the College of New Jersey (known today as Princeton) but left before graduating. That didn't stop him from getting a job at a prestigious South Carolina law firm and continuing to study law on his own. In 1797, he passed the bar exam for South Carolina but never actually practiced law.

Instead, Alston invested a large portion of his family's money into land and slaves. The investment paid off, since Joseph Alston's rice plantation made him the wealthiest man in South Carolina. Alston looked to parlay his financial success into the world of politics, but the people of South Carolina didn't like him very much.

Enter Theodosia Burr. Her and Alston discussed that a union between them could be mutually beneficial. Alston had enough money to erase Aaron Burr's debt, and the Burr name carried enough clout to sway the election in Alston's favor. The Burr-Hamilton duel had not yet taken place. Joseph Alston was rewarded with a seat in the South Carolina House of Representatives.

Soon after, Theodosia wrote to her father that while the marriage may have started out of convenience, she had formed an affection for Alston, and in 1802 the couple had a son, Aaron Burr Alston.

In 1807, when Aaron Burr was arrested for treason, Joseph Alston stood with him at his trial. Even though Aaron Burr was never found guilty of a crime, he was still forced to leave the country. During the four and a half years that Burr was in exile, Theodosia continued to send him letters and money. She also wrote letters to the secretary of the Treasury, begging for her father's return. When Thomas Jefferson left office in 1809, Theodosia also wrote letters to Dolley Madison, wife of the new president, James Madison, on her father's behalf.

Finally, in June 1812, arrangements were made for Aaron Burr's return to New York. He arrived a month later, but instead of the year of 1812 being the most joyous year of Theodosia's life, as it should have been, it turned out to be her lowest point—especially the month of June.

The first tragedy of 1812 involved her son Aaron. You see, South Carolina summers were well known for outbreaks of malaria. Back in those days, no one knew that malaria was carried by mosquitos or that the vast swamps and rice plantations of South Carolina were perfect breeding grounds for the bloodthirsty insects.

Alston had a way of protecting his plantation workers. He paid extra to have slaves brought from parts of Africa with high rates of childhood malaria, knowing that if they survived it as a child, they were less likely to suffer from it as adults. He could do little, however, to protect his own family.

Originally, Theodosia and their son spent the summer months up north with her father in New York; however, Burr's exile changed all of that. In June 1812, Aaron Burr Alston contracted malaria and passed away on June 30, ironically just two weeks before Aaron Burr's return from Europe. He was just ten years old. Her son's death and the torment that it caused her weighed heavily on Theodosia's health. This, and the state of the nation, prevented her from making the trip to welcome her father home until December 1812.

What do I mean by "the state of the nation," you may be wondering.

Following their defeat in the Revolutionary War, England sought to subvert the United States indirectly. Britain sent guns and ammo to Canada, which used them in their trade dealings with the Native Americans of the western United States. They hoped to incite a war within America so that they could swoop in on the remains.

England was also in outright conflict with France, and during the early years of the 1800s, both nations would routinely stop American ships to search for any of their own citizens who were deserting their military service. France eventually stopped this practice, but England escalated their blockades.

In 1807, a British ship fired warning shots at an American vessel. They boarded it and arrested four sailors, even though three of them were American citizens. All of the United States' efforts to negotiate their release failed. Soon Americans began to demand another war against England to redeem the nation's honor and force England to cease its hostile maritime actions.

In June, the War of 1812 began. Increased security measures due to the war and Theodosia's failing health meant that she had to postpone her trip to New York until December. By then she had recovered enough to resume overseeing the day-to-day activities of the Alston household. In early December, Joseph Alston had been appointed governor of South Carolina, so he was unable to accompany Theodosia on her journey. Alston arranged for a close friend, Timothy Green, to escort her in his stead. The governor chartered the fastest ship he could find, the *Patriot*, to carry Green, Theodosia, and her hand maiden on their journey northward. Among her chests and baggage, Theodosia brought along a portrait of herself to present to her father.

Many ships in that era were used as privateers. A privateer is when the government hires private ships to carry out military raids at sea. The *Patriot* had been operating as a privateer for several months, raiding and plundering British ships. No matter what you call them, privateers were basically government-sanctioned pirates. To conceal the *Patriot*'s recent privateering reputation, the ship was repainted and its name was changed.

On December 31, 1812, the *Patriot* left the port of Georgetown, South Carolina, and was never seen again.

Several rumors began to circulate when the schooner did not arrive at its destination. Through the years, some evidence surfaced to support many of these speculations. With each piece of alleged evidence that surfaced, historians had one more piece to the puzzle of Theodosia's disappearance. After a while, the full story could be surmised.

In the 1800s, the Carolina Bankers were *not* a financial organization. They were an outlaw group affiliated with the most notorious pirate of the day, Dominique York. The Bankers didn't have ships fast enough to chase down their prey, so they devised a brilliant, albeit cruel, plan to bring the ships to them. At low tide, the sandbanks off Nags Head were above water.

The Bankers would tie a lantern around a horse's neck, injure one of its legs, and then lead it back and forth across the sand. In the dark, the slowly bobbing light resembled a boat securely lashed to a dock. Unsuspecting ships looking for shelter and provisions would steer toward the light, thinking they had reached a port. They would then run aground on the shallow sand banks and find themselves under attack by the Bankers' ships.

All indications are that such was the fate of the *Patriot*. In three separate trials, men convicted of piracy confessed to scuttling a ship in January 1813. They said that there was a young woman on board who kept talking about going to visit her father in New York.

Also, a woman claimed that when she was young—around that same time—the body of a woman had washed ashore near her family's farm. She said that the corpse was wearing an expensive gown and showed every indication of wealth and refinement. The family buried her on their farm.

And then there is the portrait that Theodosia took with her on the schooner. In 1869, it came to be in the ownership of Dr. William Pool of Elizabeth City, although at the time he had no idea that he possessed such an important piece of history. The portrait had been given to him as payment by an old, destitute woman named Polly Tillett Mann.

According to Mann, during the War of 1812 a deserted ship drifted into port at Nags Head. The townsmen searched the derelict vessel. It had obviously been ransacked before being set adrift, and all coin, treasure, and anything of obvious worth had already been taken, but the personal effects of the crew and passengers were left behind. In the stateroom of the ship they found expensive silk dresses scattered across the floor. The pirates either had no use for such fine attire or did not know of their extreme value. The men gathered up the dresses to take to their wives and girlfriends. By the time John Tillett got to the stateroom, all the fine dresses were gone, but there was an oil painting hanging on the wall. He took the painting back to his fiancée, Polly.

The portrait hung in their home for many years. After John Tillett passed away, Polly remarried and became Polly Tillett Mann. Mann also passed away, and the elderly Mrs. Mann fell on hard times. In 1869, when Dr. Pool came to visit her, the portrait was the only thing of any value that she had left to give him.

Dr. Pool had an artist friend examine the painting, and he found it to be of a very professional style. The gown and jewels that the subject wore identified her as a woman of obvious wealth and breeding. Dr. Pool hung the portrait in his study and didn't really give it much thought until years later, when he read a magazine article about Theodosia Burr Alston and her mysterious disappearance. There was a picture that accompanied the article, and Dr. Pool felt that it very closely resembled the woman in the portrait.

Convinced that the portrait was that of Theodosia, Pool contacted as many of Burr's relatives as would listen. Many of them came to Pool's house in Elizabeth City to witness the painting for themselves. Their conclusions were indecisive. A couple of them positively identified the woman in the portrait as Theodosia, while others were not so sure, but they could not deny the striking similarity to the woman. Historians have compared the portrait to other paintings that are documented as being of Theodosia, and have acknowledged that the painting is authentic. It now hangs in Farmington, Connecticut, at the Lewis-Walpole Library of Yale University.

Even though the convicted pirates confessed to killing everyone on board the *Patriot*, there are many who say that Theodosia was taken to Bald Head Island to be held for ransom. As the daughter of the former vice president and wife of the most powerful man in South Carolina, she would have been worth more to them alive than dead.

One story goes that Theodosia was as clever as she was beautiful, and she managed to escape her captors, but she may not have realized that she was on an island. Three guards were sent to bring her back, and as they closed in on her and, having found no way off the island, Theodosia threw herself into the ocean rather than be recaptured. When the guards returned empty handed, they were beheaded. Rumor has it that the men can still be seen roaming the island in search of the young woman who had eluded them.

During World War II, the Coast Guard kept men on Bald Head Island to watch for enemy submarines. One evening, two men were patrolling on horseback when they saw a woman in the distance. The island was off-limits to civilians during those years. The trespasser wore a long, flowing, green dress and was staring out into the surf. The men yelled for her to stay where she was and identify herself. She turned toward them and disappeared into thin air!

Several days later they saw the woman again. This time she was walking slowly toward them. Unsettled, the men once more called for her to halt and identify herself, but she kept walking toward them. One of the men shouldered his rifle as the other guard demanded that the woman stop where she was. Again, she ignored their order. The man fired, and to the dismay of them both, the bullet passed right through her emerald-green dress and kicked up sand on the beach behind her.

Then, as before, she slowly faded from sight, leaving the men confused and bewildered. The next day, the men were talking about what they had seen at a bar in Southport. An elderly fisherman overheard them and asked, "So you've seen her too . . . the ghost of Theodosia Burr?"

The old man told them his story. He said he had seen the woman many years earlier, when the war was just beginning. She was in a long dress, staring out to sea. As he approached her, the woman turned to him and pointed out towards the water, in the direction that she had been looking. She seemed to be trying to tell him something, but then the man realized that he could see *through* the woman! Her green dress was not material enough to block out the driftwood lying on the beach behind her. The fisherman panicked and ran away. Back safely at home, he wondered what it was that she had been trying to tell him. The following morning, the man heard that an oil tanker had been torpedoed directly off the beach where he had seen the apparition. The man was sure that the ghost of Theodosia Burr Alston had been trying to warn him about the coming attack.

Robert Frost wrote the poem "Kitty Hawk" to commemorate the 1903 first flight of the Wright brothers. The poem is included in Frost's last book, *In the Clearing*, published in 1963. Frost wrote the poem based on the two occasions that he visited Kitty Hawk, North Carolina: once in 1894, when he was nineteen, and then again in 1953, for the fiftieth anniversary of the Wright brothers' flight.

The poem is lengthy, at 473 lines, allowing Frost to tell how he met a man in Elizabeth City who told him the story of Theodosia Burr and the Coast Guardsmen. Here is a short excerpt of the poem.

There I next fell in
With a lone coast guard
On midnight patrol,
Who as of a sect
Asked about my soul
And where-all I'd been
Apropos of sin,
Did I recollect
How the wreckers wrecked
Theodosia Burr
Off this very shore?
'Twas to punish her
But her father more—
We don't know what for:
There was no confession.
Things they think she wore
Still sometimes occur
In someone's possession
Here at Kitty Hawk.
We can have no notion
Of the strange devotion
Burr had for his daughter:
He was too devoted.

DAN'S STORY

I first learned about the mysterious disappearance of Theodosia Burr on a trip to the Outer Banks with my family several years ago. No, it wasn't while listening to *Hamilton*. I was on a walking ghost tour of Manteo with my wife and kids. I'm a big fan of walking ghost tours, and the Carolinas have some of the very best to offer. I've done tours from Asheville to Charleston, and I always jump at the chance to be a part of one. It's part of the reason why I make *The Carolina Haints Podcast* and why we're writing this book. It's one thing to read about these stories, but to actually be there and see the place, especially at night, with the shared enthusiasm and excitement of a group of like-minded strangers— well, that's my bag.

While on this ghost tour in Manteo, the guide told us a version of the story that we haven't found in our research, and I wanted to share it with you here. Poor Theodosia, desperate to spend the holidays with her father, got him to pull some strings, and he drafted a document that was signed by the governors of each state she was to pass by on her journey north. The document proclaimed that Theodosia was to travel unmolested—so when her ship was accosted off the shores of the Outer Banks, and as every single member of the *Patriot* was garroted and thrown off board to hungry sharks, she eagerly displayed her document.

The pirates, who had used the Nag's Head trick to wreck her ship, agreed to save her for last, forcing her to watch as they butchered every other passenger and crew member first. When the carnage and brutality finally came down to Theodosia, the story is she went ballistic. I try to imagine what must have been going through her head—being as smart and well educated as she, the daughter of a former vice president, and having fully expected to make her trip safely—to have to stand there and watch as person after person was murdered. Seeing the blood spill on the planks, hearing the screams and the wet gurgles of men, women, and children—this would have a profound impact on anyone.

Supposedly when they began dragging Theodosia to her death, she quite literally lost her mind and flipped out in an impressive display. Now, there's plenty of clichés about pirates, but one of the more applicable ones to this story is that they're by and large a superstitious lot. Upon seeing her dramatic change in behavior, they unhanded her and watched as she had her fit. Fearing that she might even be contagious, they let her run away for fear that she might die of something catching, as opposed to their blade.

As the legend goes, Theodosia clung to her portrait for dear life and ran onto land as fast as her feet would take her. She eventually collapsed on the sandy ground. The next day, she was found by a married couple who were out walking the beach. They could tell by her attire that she was a well-to-do woman, and since she was found in a state of shock, they felt they had no choice but to take her in. It was clear that Theodosia had suffered a profound mental breakdown and needed to be cared for. She couldn't even tell them her name. They might've assumed she was a person of some importance, but they had no clue as to her identity. The couple just knew that she needed food and shelter.

As the years passed by, the couple continued to care for Theodosia, well into her old age. You have to keep in mind that there weren't exactly a lot of options back then; no adult protective services, no nursing homes readily available. I imagine they began to think of Theodosia as a part of the family. Well, as tends to happen with old age, her health declined. Eventually the couple called for a doctor to come and check on the aged woman. Not unlike today, healthcare was expensive, and the doctor expected compensation for his services. The couple looked around and finally offered the doctor the one thing they knew Theodosia had in her possession—the portrait.

Nag's Head Portrait (Theodosia Burr). Courtesy of the
Lewis Walpole Library, Yale University

The doctor, seeing that the painting was one of high quality and potentially high value, agreed to accept Theodosia's portrait as payment. Finally, after years of catatonia, silence, and infirmness, the elderly woman stood up and loudly proclaimed, "I am Theodosia Burr!" The woman picked up her feet and ran out the front door, across the sand, and straight into the Atlantic Ocean, where she drowned.

This was the story as relayed by the tour guide as we looked out across Shallowbag Bay at Festival Park. As you may have imagined, this story caught my attention and sparked my imagination. I began devouring as much information as I could find on the disappearance of Theodosia. I'm aware that the bulk of the research suggests she simply drowned in a shipwreck. Plenty of old pirates have also been said to have made the deathbed confession of being present during her execution. There are even theories that she was held for ransom somewhere in the West Indies; however, this version, since I was first told it by a professional storyteller, is my favorite.

The legend continued that Theodosia can be seen wandering the coast along with the ghostly image of the glowing Nag's Head. The story that Aaron Burr considered to be the truth behind his daughter's disappearance was that it was a shipwreck in which all members simply died at sea. Burr could never wrap his head around the idea that his daughter may have survived and was being held captive by ravenous pirates. Perhaps it was simply easier to believe that she had just passed away.

As a father, I'd do anything for my children. I realize how cliché that sounds, but I mean it in the most literal of ways. I can't imagine simply accepting news that my child had disappeared, and choosing to believe they had died, to spare myself further hard feelings. By all accounts, Aaron and Theodosia were extremely close. Their love and the potential he saw in her was even the inspiration for the musical piece "Dear Theodosia," a lovely song by Lin-Manuel Miranda. So, I can't help but wonder why he didn't use what little clout he had left, although at this point I don't imagine it was much, to go in search of her.

How could a father who had such a close bond with his daughter just accept her disappearance, fraught with as much mystery as it produced? From what we know about Aaron Burr, he was a bit of a bastard and generally known to look out for himself above all else, even over his sworn oath to his country. Trust me, the irony's not lost on me that a long-descendent nephew of Aaron Burr is now a United States senator from North Carolina and, as I write this, is currently under criminal investigation for securities fraud and insider trading. I guess he comes by it honestly.

CHAPTER 19

The Lost Colony and the White Deer of Roanoke

Manteo, North Carolina

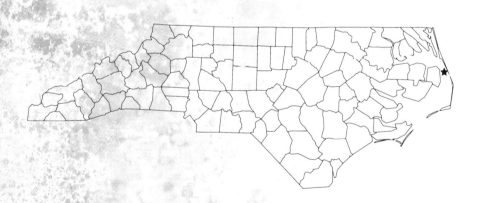

PODCAST • SEASON 2 • EPISODE 14
(March 8, 2019)

The story of the Lost Colony is well known in this area. I remember learning about it in school at a fairly young age.

Way back in 1584, Sir Walter Raleigh was assigned the task of establishing British colonies in the Americas. He sent out exploratory missions to pick some prime locations for future settlements. One of those teams identified Roanoke Island. Roanoke is about 20 miles north of Hatteras Island on the North Carolina Outer Banks, but at that time, North Carolina hadn't even been formed yet. The land was part of the colony of Virginia.

The Outer Banks was home to several Native American tribes. The exploration team established a friendship with these tribes and even brought two men back to England to describe the politics and geography of the region to Raleigh personally. The two Native Americans were named Manteo and Wanchese, and they both have towns named after them on the island.

A year later, convinced that Roanoke would be an ideal settlement location, Sir Walter Raleigh sent a small contingent of men to the island to build a fort and prepare for a larger colony. The group managed to erect the fort, but they also managed to upset the Native Americans. The small colony was low on supplies and now became the target of periodic attacks.

In 1587, Raleigh decided to cut his losses on Roanoke and proposed a new settlement in the Chesapeake Bay area. He chose his good friend, John White, to lead 115 colonists to the New World. They were to stop at Roanoke, collect the smaller group, and sail on to Chesapeake.

Among the colonists chosen were White's daughter, Eleanor, and her husband, Ananias Dare. The two had been married the year before, and Eleanor was pregnant.

They arrived at Fort Roanoke on July 22, 1587. There was no sign of the men who were supposed to be there. The fort was abandoned. The only thing they found was one, solitary skeleton. But, inexplicably, White decided to stay at Roanoke rather than continue north to Chesapeake.

Perhaps it was a decision of convenience. Why find a new location and build another fort when there's a perfectly good fort right here? Or perhaps it was for a more personal reason—after all, it was July on the Outer Banks, and Eleanor was now eight months pregnant.

The first thing John White did was to try to reestablish a truce with the Native Americans. It wasn't an easy task, but at the end of the day, White was able to institute a tenuous friendship with the tribes.

Or so he thought.

Just a couple of weeks later, that friendship would become untwined. A man named George Howe was out alone collecting crabs when he was killed by one of the Native American tribes. And just like that, the fort was once again under attack. The colonists begged John White to return to England and bring back some soldiers to help them.

If you're like me, you're probably wondering right now why they didn't just all pile on the ship and head to Chesapeake per the original orders. But . . . they didn't.

And in the midst of all this fear and turmoil, on August 18, Eleanor Dare gave birth to a baby girl. They named her Virginia, after the territory. Virginia Dare was the first European born in North America.

A few days later, on August 25, White consented and set sail for England, but as fate would have it, he arrived home to find violence on the home front as well. England was in the middle of the Anglo-Spanish War, and the queen had commandeered every able ship for the war effort.

White was left stranded. In August 1590, after a three-year absence, he finally made it back to Roanoke. There was no sign of his daughter or his granddaughter, or of the other 116 souls he had left behind. The only clue was carved into the trunk of a nearby tree: the word . . .

CROATOAN.

This was confusing. He had left the colonists with a signal to be used in case they were forced to flee; they were to carve a Maltese cross into a tree or post. Since they didn't do that, John White assumed that they left by choice. The fort itself bolstered this hypothesis. All the houses and the fortifications were gone. If the Native Americans had killed everyone, they would have most likely burned the fort or simply destroyed everything. But it appeared to White that the buildings had been systematically dismantled and moved.

White came to the conclusion that the settlement must have decided to relocate to Croatoan Island (now known as Hatteras Island). But he was unable to search any further. A storm was coming in, and his men refused to sail in the harsh weather. The following day they returned to England.

John White implored Sir Walter Raleigh to send another search party, but rescue missions weren't very profitable, so Raleigh refused. White died in 1593, never having seen his family again.

In 1602, nine years after White's death, and at least twelve years since the colony's disappearance, Raleigh sent Samuel Mace to Roanoke Island. Their mission: to gather exotic plants and wood that could be sold at a profit back in England . . . and if there's time, keep an eye out for those lost colonists. Needless to say, they did not find anything.

Another lesser-known legend also surrounds the fate of the Lost Colony and Virginia Dare.

Remember Manteo and Wanchese, who came back to England at the beginning of the story? This legend pits Wanchese as the villain. Having seen London and how the Europeans exploited and mistreated nature, he plotted against the Roanoke colony. Shortly after John White set sail for home, Wanchese launched his attack. He and his warriors killed every one of them. Only the Dare family survived.

Some versions say that Ananias, Eleanor, and Virginia Dare ran away and were taken in by Manteo, who was now chief of the Croatan tribe. Other versions claim that only Eleanor and Virginia escaped and that Ananias was shot by Wanchese when he stopped to carve CROATOAN in a tree trunk.

Either way, Virginia survives and grows up with the Croatan, who call her Winona. Manteo took her under his wing, and she learned the ways of the forest. She became the most beautiful maiden in the village, and many young braves vied for her hand, but the two biggest rivals were Okisko and Chico, the medicine man. When she chose Okisko, Chico began to plot his revenge. If he couldn't have her, no one could.

In the evenings, Virginia would often walk at the forest's edge, along the shore of the sound. One evening, Chico followed her and cast a powerful spell on her, turning her into a snow-white doe. She ran off into the woods, afraid and alone. The village became alarmed when she didn't return home. They searched for her for days. Finally, they assumed that she must have drowned in the sound.

During the years that followed, the white doe was often seen walking along the edge of the forest or prancing around the ruins of old Fort Roanoke, but no one realized that the doe was actually Virginia Dare.

That is, until Okiska, heartbroken over the disappearance of his love, traveled to Lake Mattamusket to visit a very powerful medicine man named Wenaudon. The medicine man told him what Chico had done, and gave him an arrow with an oystershell tip. The old man cast a spell on the arrow and told Okiska that it would break the spell if he shot her with it.

But Chico found out that Okiska had learned how to bring Virginia back, and . . . knowing Wanchese's hatred of the Europeans . . . told him about the doe's true identity. Wanchese had learned that silver could kill magical creatures back in London. He melted down some silver coins and coated one of his arrowheads in it.

Both Wanchese and Okiska stalked through the forest, searching for the doe. It was getting near dawn when the doe stepped out of the trees into a clearing. It approached a creek and bent for a drink of water. Both warriors spotted the doe at the same time, from opposite sides. One consumed by hate; the other fueled by love. They notched their arrow and drew their bows. The only sound was the twang of their bowstrings as each arrow flew toward its target. The arrows struck home simultaneously.

The doe let out a single bleat. As dawn broke the horizon, a gray mist formed, concealing the animal. Okiska rushed toward the doe. When the mist cleared, he found the body of Virginia Dare. He took her in his arms and then he saw the second arrow. Wanchese stood over them and laughed as the life ebbed from her body.

She was dead.

Okiska buried her near the remains of Fort Roanoke.

To this very day, from time to time, a hunter or a tourist will emerge from the forests of Roanoke Island claiming that they saw a strange white deer. They try to hunt the animal, but it always eludes them. Residents of the island often tell them that they are not the first. And that the white deer is the ghost of Virginia Dare.

Many rumors surround the disappearance of the Lost Colony. The most widely accepted explanation came in 1607, after the settlement of Jamestown had been established. Captain John Smith interviewed the chief of the Powhatan tribe, who claimed to have led the raiding party that killed the colonists himself. He said that his priests had prophesied that he would be killed by the Chesepian tribe from that region. So, he massacred every Chesepian village he could find, including a group of Europeans that they found living among them.

DAN'S STORY

I've been fortunate to have made several trips to the Outer Banks of North Carolina. Every time I'm able to make the five-hour-plus journey, I find myself more and more in love with the place. I don't know what it is exactly that I find myself so compelled by. Perhaps it's the small-town atmosphere, or the close-knit geography. I think it has to do with the feeling of mystery that somehow permeates the air. After all, this was the place where in the late 1500s a group of British colonists came and disappeared without a trace.

Roanoke Island is one of my favorite places in the Old North State. The North Carolina Aquarium is a must-see attraction for visitors, not to mention the beautiful Elizabethan Gardens. I've even found myself, late at night, driving through the old residential neighborhoods that surround the northern end of the island, lost in thought about what it must have been like for the colonists who came here looking for a new home. It must have been a mix of excitement and fear, an existential terror that filled the hearts of every man and woman. I think about the anxiety evoked by expecting a child in 2020, with the best healthcare in history, and then strip all of that away and imagine carrying the baby that would be the first European born in the New World. Did Eleanor Dare have any sense of the history that sat on her shoulders? Or was she just concerned with the constant battle to survive?

If you find yourself in the Outer Banks of North Carolina as a visitor, your car will likely stand out from the natives with license plates that start with OBX. But that's okay; it's a region that thrives on tourism. Not only can you find some of the best seafood on the Eastern Seaboard, there's so much to see and do there— from a visit to the desertlike dunes of Jokey's Ridge State Park, to the iconic lighthouses that span the banks from north to south. You can take a ferry to Ocracoke Island and explore. You can go to the national park at Kitty Hawk and actually walk the stretch of land where Wilbur and Orville Wright first took flight. Even out of peak tourism season, if you happen to be in the area for Halloween, then Kill Devil Hills doesn't disappoint either. If you ask me, you're cheating yourself out of a wonderful experience if you don't go to Fort Raleigh and take in a performance of *The Lost Colony*.

Pick up a book of ghost and folklore tales, preferably by my favorite North Carolina ghost author, Charles H. Whedbee, and settle into some great writing to put you into the proper mood. Believe it or not, in the picturesque setting, there's more mystery than meets the eye. There's more than just the Lost Colony of Roanoke to whet your appetite. Hell, the Lost Colony isn't even the only settlement in the area to go missing (okay, perhaps "abandoned" is a better word). A little farther west from Roanoke Island, past Manns Harbor in Dare County, was a logging community called Buffalo City. About a hundred years ago, the community was home to about 3,000 citizens, an industrial mill, a school, businesses, and

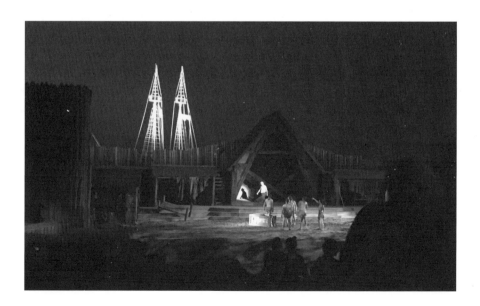

moonshining operations. Nowadays, about the only thing left to see is a road sign that reads "Buffalo City Road" at the intersection of Highway 64 at the head of the Alligator River National Wildlife Refuge.

It was once a vibrant town, the largest in the county, and the residents made their living off logging and moonshining. During the Prohibition era, business was booming! Speakeasies all over the region sold spirits made in Buffalo City; however, when Prohibition was lifted in 1933, it hit the town pretty hard. The next decade saw the town's population decimated by a few epidemics of some nasty diseases. Finally, the closing of the lumber mill was the final nail in the coffin. The town was deserted in the 1950s. All that was left of Buffalo City were the train tracks and abandoned homes and buildings. Even those have been stripped and pilfered over the years.

There aren't many photographs of the place, and most of the residents are either dead or getting up there in age. Buffalo City is a place becoming lost to time, since each year the land where the town used to sit becomes a little more grown up and wild. Pretty soon, there may not be anything left to tell anyone that a town once existed; however, the name is kept alive by the Buffalo City Mug Shop, a homegrown brewery in nearby Kill Devil Hills. There's also the award-winning short horror film *Lost in Buffalo City*, which finds its main character taking a trip to the elusive area in search of a mystery and finding more than he bargained for. It's a cool film, but I wouldn't recommend trying it for yourself.

CHAPTER 20

Blackbeard and the Cursed Town of Bath

Bath, North Carolina

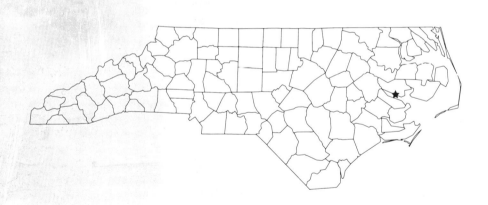

PODCAST • SEASON 3 • EPISODE 2
(October 4, 2019)

Bath is the oldest town in North Carolina. Located on a peninsula between Back and Bath Creeks in Beaufort County, it was incorporated in 1705. It served as the first capital of North Carolina, and the colonial assembly met there on several occasions. The colonial assembly was our form of national government prior to our independence in the Revolutionary War.

A decade later, Bath had a population of just 300, but it entertained at least that many more visitors at any one time. Bath was a prominent stop on the post road that ran from Portland, Maine, to Savannah, Georgia. It was also a popular port destination for traders. With such a large migrant population, Bath quickly fell into a state of near lawlessness. Saloons and brothels could be found on virtually every street. This atmosphere attracted Bath's most famous resident, Edward Teach.

Edward Teach (also known as Blackbeard—the most famous pirate the world has ever known) built a house in Bath. It was right across the creek from Governor Charles Eden's house. Now, here I should point out that the town of Beaufort also claims to have a "Blackbeard's House." And it would seem that since Bath is in Beaufort County, the two towns should be in proximity to one another, but in reality, they are not. The town of Beaufort is in Carteret County, 90 miles south of Bath. While Blackbeard did spend a considerable amount of time in Beaufort, his home was in Bath.

This was possibly because the pirate seemed to be friends (and maybe even business partners) with Governor Eden. There are even rumors that Blackbeard courted Eden's daughter, but other records indicate that Eden died childless, so those rumors may be just that . . . rumors.

In June 1718, Blackbeard was at the height of his career. He commanded a small armada of ships and more than 300 men. So, he began perhaps his most ambitious campaign. He laid siege to the city of Charleston, South Carolina. He had enough ships to blockade the entire harbor, and for about a week he demanded food, money, supplies, and women.

When he left Charleston, he did something rather unexpected. He sailed back to Bath and surrendered himself to his friend, Governor Eden. You see, the British authorities had issued a proclamation saying any pirate who surrendered by July 10 would receive the King's pardon for the crime of piracy. The catch was that most pirates were wanted for more than just piracy, but Blackbeard was smart. His buddy the governor exonerated him from any other crimes, and at the end of June 1718, Edward Teach became a free man. He settled down at his house in Bath and took a new wife . . . his fourteenth!

But he didn't stay retired for very long. Within two months he took to piracy once again, except he didn't consider it piracy. He saw himself as sort of a Robin Hood. He had enough money; he was just in it for the thrills.

He began terrorizing the surrounding colonies and bringing his spoils back to North Carolina. There he would sell his cache to the people at a greatly reduced price. Of course, his friend the governor got first pick of the bounty. In exchange, Eden kept quiet about Blackbeard's actions.

But nothing stays a secret forever, especially something like piracy. And no matter how Blackbeard saw himself, the British Crown saw him as a pirate who had broken his oath of surrender. Lieutenant Robert Maynard and a fleet of ships were dispatched to hunt him down. On November 22, 1718, Maynard defeated Blackbeard's men and beheaded Edward Teach on Ocracoke Island.

Blackbeard's death did nothing to slow the town's love of sin and excess. It was a modern-day Sodom and Gomorrah, or, as one man put it, "You will never find a more wretched hive of scum and villainy." During that time, the Great Awakening—a widespread Christian revival movement—was making its way through the colonies. In 1734, St. Thomas Episcopal Church was built in Bath, and it remains the oldest extant church in North Carolina, but the church needed some help if it was going to convert the seedy residents of Bath.

George Whitefield was a young, charismatic preacher who traveled from state to state advocating the morals of the Great Awakening. He was the Billy Graham of his day. It is estimated that Whitefield preached the Good Word to a total of ten *million* people throughout his lifetime. Whitefield visited Bath at least four times through the 1750s and up until 1762. He condemned the town's love of drinking, cussing, and dancing as works of the devil, but the town folk considered him a crackpot.

Whitefield traveled with a coffin in the back of his wagon. When questioned, he simply said that if the worst was to befall him, he wanted to make sure he had a box to be buried in. But then it was discovered that Whitefield slept in the coffin so he wouldn't have to listen to the sounds of the very vices that he preached against through the thin hotel walls . . . well, even the clergy of Bath found that to be freaking weird. On his last visit in 1762, he was told he would no longer be allowed to preach in Bath.

The fire-and-damnation preacher was outraged. He stopped his wagon at the edge of town, took off his shoes, and dusted them off. He said, "There's a place in the Bible that says if a place won't listen to the Word and you shake the dust of the town off your feet, then the town shall be cursed. I say to the village of Bath, you shall remain, now and forever, forgotten by men and nations until such time as it pleases God to turn the light of His countenance again upon you!" And so, the curse was made.

Did it work? Well today, Bath actually has a *lower* population than it had 300 years ago. Most say this is a coincidence. After the death of Blackbeard and the election of a new governor, the state capital was moved to New Bern, and, it seemed, the rest of North Carolina was eager to distance themselves from the Sodom and Gomorrah of the Carolinas.

But whispers of the curse were renewed when, fifty years later, the devil himself paid Bath a visit.

In 1813, Jesse Elliot was a horse-racing enthusiast. Even though it was illegal to do such things on the Sabbath, Jesse and his friends didn't much care. Jesse was known as a rough character, and he would often get drunk and disrupt Sunday church services with his vile cursing, just for spite. He and the others met most Sunday afternoons to see whose horse was the fastest, and to drink and do whatever the hell they felt like doing. And Jesse knew that he had the fastest horse in the county.

One morning, a mysterious stranger rode into town on a jet-black stallion and challenged him to a race; Jesse eagerly accepted. They agreed on a $100 wager and met at the track later that day. Jesse's buddies gathered around to egg him on and place bets among themselves. Soon the two men lined up on the starting line . . . and were off!

Jesse whipped and cursed at his horse, squeezing every last drop of speed out of him. It seemed to work—he pulled ahead. But he didn't ease up. On and on he drove his horse, and his lead lengthened. The stranger didn't seem bothered by what everyone agreed was an insurmountable lead. On the backstretch, Jesse was heard to yell: "Take me a winner or take me to hell!" And still the stranger remained unfazed as Jesse continued to pull ahead.

But as Jesse rounded the final turn on the way to sure victory, his horse caught a glimpse of the mysterious stranger behind them. No one knows what or whom the horse saw there, but the sight frightened him so much that he stopped dead. He slammed down his mighty hooves, sinking them a few inches into the ground and throwing Jesse through the air. He "landed" headfirst into a pine tree, killing him instantly. The stranger never slowed a bit; he kept riding on past Jesse's body. Witnesses claim that the stranger was laughing maniacally as he crossed the finish line, sped past them, and rode off into the woods . . . never to be seen again.

It was claimed that bits of Jesse Elliot's hair and scalp were stuck in the tree for months because the locals were too superstitious to remove them. And the locals had good reason to be superstitious. It didn't take them long to realize that the gouges in the earth made by Jesse Elliot's horse didn't erode away or fill in like normal holes do. They tried to fill them in themselves, but the next day the holes were found just as fresh and clear of debris as the day they were made.

And today, 200 years later, if you visit the site yourself, they are still there. They are located in a grassy area, yet no grass grows in the holes. Needles from the nearby pine trees litter the ground, but the holes remain clean. It is still believed that if you try to fill in the holes, they will be pristine a few hours later.

A news crew visited the site once. They heard stories about livestock who were feeding from the area and wouldn't eat anything from within the marks. So they borrowed some chickens, bought some feed, and set up their cameras. They scattered the feed both inside and outside the holes. The chickens greedily attacked the feed surrounding the holes. When they had eaten all of it, they stood on the edge of the holes and eyed the feed within the depressions. But none of them would eat from them or even step foot down into the holes.

The owner of the property told them that the area had once been used to house hogs. The animals churned up the earth into a muddy pulp with their heavy hooves and rutting around. All trace of the mysterious hoofprints was obliterated. But, he said, when the hogs were removed from the land and the land was given time to recover, the strange marks returned, exactly as they had been.

Before they left, the news crew tested one more claim. They filled the holes with dirt, leaves, and small stones. Then they covered the whole thing with a network of threads, so if anyone tried to tamper with it, the delicate threads would break. When they returned the following morning, the holes were clear, and the threads were still intact.

A group of scientists from Duke University investigated the holes but found no definitive cause for the anomaly. The prevailing scientific theory is that they are a result of groundwater, or veins of salt, or very small sinkholes . . . or a 300-year-old curse.

DAN'S STORY

Before embarking on the three-hour-plus trip to Bath, I made sure to do some research on the location of the Devil's Hoofprints. Not surprisingly, several sites on the internet claim to have the location and even GPS coordinates. One source said that there was a small patch of old crumbly concrete where a roadside gift shop once stood that marks the spot. I researched the area thoroughly and even attempted to make contact with the owners of the property, to no avail. So when the governor's first phase of the COVID-19 stay-at-home order was lifted, I took the first opportunity I had to get myself to Bath. Fortunately, my father came with me.

As we turned onto Camp Leach Road from Highway 264/92, headed toward Goose Creek State Park, I had no idea whether or not it would be a wasted trip. The surroundings we encountered were a little bit different from the way Google Maps had it recorded. According to my research, the part where I thought the hoofprints were located looked a bit different than they did in person. So it became obvious that I wasn't going to be able to simply pull over and just take a quick, inconspicuous look. I'm also not comfortable just walking into a stranger's yard, so it looked like I was going to have to knock on the door and ask for permission. This is the uncomfortable part of writing this book. I don't enjoy knocking on a stranger's door. I don't like when strangers knock on my door, but we just drove a considerable distance to get there, and I wasn't about to let a little thing like my own discomfort stand in the way. So I sucked it up and decided to knock. So far, while researching this book, folks have been pretty accommodating and welcoming. Thankfully, so were these people. I parked in the driveway, and before I could ring the doorbell, I was met by the resident. I greeted her friendly and was relieved to see she returned my greeting with her own warmness. I explained to her that I'm writing a book about North Carolina folklore and was wondering if she was familiar with the hoofprints. A look of amusement and recognition washed across the face of Sherry Dodge.

Dodge explained, "I just moved here in December, but I have had a couple of people stop by looking for them. They're supposed to be right here [indicating her house]. Some kids came up with their dad and asked me if they could walk around the property, and I was like, 'Yeah, sure, whatever.' They even had pictures made in the yard. I don't know the whole story on that, but help yourself to walk around, look around; I understand that they're supposed to be somewhere in this general area, near the little dirt road with a gate. So feel free to do whatever you need to do."

Flabbergasted by Sherry's generosity, I graciously accepted her consent and didn't give her a chance to change her mind. We started off walking down the side of Camp Leach Road, toward Goose Creek Road. We came across a sandy dirt road with an old rusty gate. Sherry said she thought this might have something to do with it. I found two small, poorly defined paths that led to virtually nowhere. I found a little white patch on the ground that might be where the concrete area may have been. Behind was just the hint of a footpath, so I began following it a ways into the woods.

I was just looking for anything I could find. I found a few small, bare patches of earth. I was not trying to wander too far off from the dirt road, because I didn't know if I was in the right spot, and I didn't want to get lost. I encountered some

sort of peculiar droppings from a large animal, perhaps a bear, and determined this first spot was a lost cause. I returned to the dirt road empty-handed. I found yet another small footpath along the other side of the dirt road. After a brief exploration, I found that also to be a lost cause. So I decided to get back onto the road and make my way back down toward the house.

Now here's where things start to get weird. As we walked back, I felt compelled to look over to my right while passing a small opening in the woods, about 50 feet from the road, at the wood line. At this point, I thought, "I'm just pulling at straws here, but I haven't found anything yet. What've I got to lose?" I jumped the ditch and approached the wood line, only to find at the opening Dad pointing out that someone has marked the spot with a little yellow plastic tag, about 7 feet high. As you can imagine, my excitement level grew exponentially. If someone had taken the time to place a marker, then either it was totally coincidental or it was put there so someone could find it again.

We pushed farther into the woods, about 50 feet in, and that's when I spotted it. I saw the metal cord running low to the ground, which had been placed there to cordon it off. The cord was held in place by a series of wooden posts in the ground. I knew that someone a long time ago roped off the area, but I had no idea the size of the diameter, which was about 25 feet across. I couldn't help but be reminded of my multiple trips to the Devil's Tramping Ground.

I stepped inside the circle. Once inside, my vision was immediately drawn to a deep depression toward the middle. It was about a foot to a foot and a half in diameter and was composed mostly of a dark-gray, sandy soil. There was a little bit of debris, including two small sticks that someone had placed in the middle to mark it. I looked around, and it took me a few minutes before I realized that the Devil's Hoofprints were actually the Devil's Hoofprint, as in *singular*. There were no other deep depressions in the ground that were in any way similar to the apparent one. Sure, I found a few places here and there that looked as if it could be right, but nothing like this one.

I took a few quick photographs of the hoofprint and its surroundings. And I simply spent some time within the boundaries before moving on. There was a large tree stump just outside the circle, which I couldn't help but think might be where Jesse Elliot met his demise. I returned to Sherry's house and was able to meet her adult son, Tanner, who turned out to be just as nice as his mother. I told them both of my findings, and they were excited. Sherry said that when they moved in, they were told that the property was legendary, but they didn't quite understand how. Sherry had done only a cursory amount of research on the internet and was mainly familiar with the Devil's Hoofprints in England.

I told Sherry and Tanner a bit about the legend in their own backyard and offered to show Tanner myself so they could find it too. Tanner was eager to see the site for himself and seemed pretty impressed that he'd been living with such a legend for six months and didn't know anything about it. I encouraged Tanner and Sherry to check out the episode of the podcast about the story and to read up about it from multiple literary sources.

I can't thank Sherry and Tanner enough for their warmth and hospitality. They could have easily told me to get off the property and kept a closed mind to the very notion of the story, but I found them to be very kind and receptive and, best of all, curious. If you're reading this and feel compelled to go see the hoofprint for yourself, please be mindful of their privacy and respect their wishes. This is private property, after all. As much as you may feel you're entitled to see this thing up close, I assure you, you're not.

If you are able to go, with the blessings of the current resident, keep an open mind. Don't litter. Don't start any fires. Don't make the mistake of trying to take a piece of it with you. That's a common mistake many people make upon visiting a site of supernatural significance. And it's usually one they tend to regret.

After making the discovery, we decided to go explore the small town of Bath. While I must say it is a pretty little town, it is certainly very small. We were fortunate to be able to make the trip soon after the quarantine order was lifted, but there still wasn't much to see. I was expecting to see a small coastal community, for sure, but one with ample tourism activities. I found only one open antique and gift shop and one open restaurant. We happily patronized both establishments and ate a meal of fried pork chops while overlooking the waters at Bonner's Point Bay, facing the home of Edward Teach.

What Bath does have a lot of is historical places—and it absolutely should. After all, it's the first established town in the state of North Carolina. It seems like every corner you turn, there's a beautiful and historic landmark. I got the impression that there must be more state historical markers per capita than any other town. I recall seeing four or five within eyeshot of each other. We were able to visit St. Thomas Episcopal Church and its small graveyard. The historical marker advised that the church was the "oldest church building in the state of North Carolina, constructed in 1734." Built just two years prior was the Queen Anne—the bell of St. Thomas Church, which stood on display right next to the building. A marker advised that the Queen Anne "was cast in England in 1732 and recast in Troy, N.Y. in 1872. Is said to have been purchased with funds from Queen Anne's Bounty, and has been in continuous use through the years." As is a common theme with my research, I wish I could have spent more time there exploring, but we did have a lovely afternoon in Bath and found it a place that I'd love to revisit.

Now, for the really weird part. I've been able to retain so much information and write about encounters and thoughts with so much detail because I've utilized a small digital recorder throughout my research. I always thought it was such a cliché for writers to talk into a personal recorder and play back the audio while writing, but I decided to give it a shot when my research team made our first trip. And boy, how I've enjoyed using it. I've been able to write about all kinds of specific little details that I would surely have forgotten without it. It's been a lifesaver, and I've taken this little device all over the state of North Carolina, from one edge to another, and it's always been a reliable tool. I even used it when exploring Bath and meeting Sherry Dodge. The thing worked perfectly ... except when I turned the recorder back on and decided to approach the path that led me to the Devil's Hoofprint itself. My recording is inexplicably gone. I have an MP3 file that shows a recording took place, with the date and time, but try as I might, I have not been able to get the file to play.

I'm not the kind of person who goes into something like this expecting to have some sort of technical difficulty because of spirits. But I'm also not the kind of person to dismiss something like this as a simple glitch. It's not lost on me that many paranormal researchers report finding a sudden loss in battery or missing footage as a somewhat common occurrence when exploring haunted sites. Who knows? Maybe it is a weird coincidence that my tried-and-true device finally decided to crap the bed when I needed it most. But I do think it's odd that recordings I made on the same day, prior to and after stepping foot within the circle, came out just fine. As I've said before, it's not my intention to look for or report any supernatural findings, but it is what it is.

These things happened. Make up your own mind.

AFTERWORD

BY DAN SELLERS

There's a recurring theme in ghost stories that we've touched on a bit in this book, and that's regarding anniversaries. It's often said that spirits will return to a special place on the same day every year. In some cases, it's on a cold, rainy night, similar to the conditions that are somehow important in telling their story. It's an odd thing and hard to reconcile with a logical mind—that ghosts would choose to reappear on a specific day. We tend to think of ghosts almost as an omniscient presence, capable of appearing anywhere and anytime, to whomever they choose, seemingly at their own free will. But perhaps, like life itself, it's a little more complicated than that.

It was after nine o'clock at night when I slipped on a pair of boots, grabbed a flashlight and my digital recorder, and headed out the door, leaving my wife alone with two kids and a newborn. What on earth would have compelled me to take a ride at this hour, on this date? The answer is this afterword portion of the book. You see, if you'll recall back to the previous chapter on Lydia, the Hitchhiking Ghost of Jamestown, then you'll

perhaps know that it's a special night. June 20, 2020, marks the one hundredth anniversary of the night Annie Luda Jackson was killed on the roadside near the infamous bridge in Jamestown.

According to Michael Renegar and Amy Greer's book *Looking for Lydia*, Jackson is the poor soul who has been immortalized throughout history as the apparition herself. In some versions of the story, Lydia appears to traveling motorists on the anniversary of her death. In other versions, the date appears to be more or less random, but coinciding with a cold and rainy night. It was reported that the fatal crash occurred at approximately 10 p.m. on June 20, 1920. If I was quick enough, I could get to the scene of the crash in time.

Weather reports from a week prior predicted rain on the evening of June 20, 2020. I bought myself a brand-new poncho just for the occasion; however, when the evening rolled around, it was as dry as a bone. The thermometer registered about 73 degrees, a reasonable temperature for the first day of summer. While the heat was certainly tolerable, the humidity caused my glasses to fog upon exiting my vehicle. I made it to the infamous bridge at 9:45 p.m. After making a pass through and coming back around, I parked on the side of the road, near a newly made construction access.

There were numerous large pieces of construction equipment along the side of the road and small patch of land in between the road and the old underpass, better known as Lydia's bridge. I made my way through the dark, past the equipment, and onto the bridge. Immediately I saw several lights inside and the glow of not one but two cell phones. I assumed ahead of time that it was reasonably likely other folks would make the trip to this destination, on this particular night—and I was right. Fully understanding that a dark figure approaching might seem frightening or even threatening, I greeted the strangers warmly and asked if they were here for the anniversary. The two gentlemen agreed and told me they made the trip together to be here on this special night.

The two were from around Fayetteville, Hope Mills to be exact. They told me they had visited the bridge several times over the years. They said that once, a few years ago, they found a spirit board table with a plastic disc tied to the table, presumably to be used as a planchette, and that the letters appeared to have been hand-painted on the tabletop. I recalled the makeshift Ouija I found on a long-ago visit, and looked around the interior walls of the bridge for new graffiti. The two gentlemen never specifically said they were amateur ghost hunters or anything like that, but that's certainly the vibe I got from them. They said that they heard three knocking noises coming from above them earlier in the night, but couldn't provide an explanation for its source. One of them told me about a similar haunting at Fayetteville's Prince Charles Hotel involving the ghost of a young girl in a flowing white dress.

According to the guys, around 10:15 they planned to kill their lights and quiet down to listen out for Lydia. They believed Lydia was killed in the crash at precisely 10:38 p.m. I asked them where they got that information and why they were so sure of the time, but they didn't know, or at least they weren't willing to share. However, the gentlemen were willing to share a beer from their cooler. I declined but made sure to introduce myself and shake their hands. I then politely excused myself to go scout other spots along this haunted area, solo.

I made my way to the top of the steep hill and sat along the concrete wall that overlooks East Main Street. I took a seat and just sat there, taking in the quiet and stillness of the night. I looked down at the same stretch of road where Tom Beasley said he encountered the image of a stranded girl in the pouring rain in 1972. I surveyed the whole area, from the nearby parking lot at GTCC (where a campus police officer was checking out the car of my new friends), to the town's construction equipment, to the old underpass itself. I tried to imagine what the macadam road would have looked like back then, with the upside-down automobile in the torrential downpour.

At 10:31, I heard what distinctly sounded like a woman shrieking. It was faint, and in the distance, farther east than where I was, from the direction of the old underpass. I heard only one remote cry, and anything else that might've been heard was drowned out by bullfrogs croaking, the chirping of nocturnal critters, and the excessively loud noise of passing motorists. Nothing about the scream sounded *otherworldly* or otherwise unnatural. For all I know, it was an upset neighbor at the nearby apartment complex. Or it could have been the two ghost hunters from Fayetteville, hootin' and hollerin' in the tunnel. The most likely explanation was that my imagination was helping my eager brain fill in some empty gaps, and I simply misinterpreted a natural noise for a woman's deathly shriek.

Shortly before leaving, I encountered a whole family of folks who came walking up the road on foot. There was a man, three women, and a child, carrying a flashlight. They made it all the way to the foot of the hill, at the top of which I was standing, rather creepily, I might add. Upon shining their light in my direction and suffering the initial shock of seeing someone standing in the dark, I politely asked them if they were here for the anniversary, to which they agreed. I gave them directions on how to get to the bridge on foot, and they made their way to join the others.

Upon getting back in the car, I drove slowly back and forth a few times, just to see if there was anything to see. I never saw the pale figure of a lovely apparition on the side of the road. Nor did I truly expect to. I think the explorer in me simply couldn't pass up the opportunity to be there for the very moment the one hundredth anniversary took place. I always try to visit these places without expectations. I suppose if I judged success in terms of seeing a ghost, or having a supernatural experience, then I'd probably be pretty let down. That's not how I look at it though. For me, there's power in the connection I can make between hearing the story and standing in the spot.

If you've read this book hoping to hear tales of my heroic encounters with the paranormal, then I'm sorry to have disappointed you. Through this collection of stories, I simply hope that I've entertained you. If I'm lucky, perhaps it will inspire you to go visit some spooky places yourself and make your own adventures.

Who knows?

Maybe you'll have your own story to tell.

SELECT BIBLIOGRAPHY

Bane, Theresa. *Haunted Historic Greensboro*. Atglen, PA: Schiffer, 2009.

Barefoot, Daniel W. *North Carolina's Haunted Hundred*. Vol. 1, *Seaside Spectres*. Winston-Salem, NC: John F. Blair, 2002a.

Barefoot, Daniel W. *North Carolina's Haunted Hundred*. Vol. 2, *Piedmont Phantoms*. Winston-Salem, NC: John F. Blair, 2002b.

Brickner, Michael. *Haunted Winston-Salem*. Haunted America. Charleston, SC: Arcadia, 2015.

Calloway, Burt, and Jennifer FitzSimons. *Triad Hauntings: Ghost Stories from Winston-Salem, Greensboro, High Point, and Surrounding Areas*. Winston-Salem, NC: Bandit Books, 1990.

Casstevens, Frances H. *Ghosts of the North Carolina Piedmont: Haunted Houses and Unexplained Events*. Haunted America. Charleston, SC: Arcadia, 2009.

Hairr, John. *Monsters of North Carolina: Mysterious Creatures in the Tar Heel State*. Mechanicsburg, PA: Stackpole Books, 2013.

Hall, Lynne L. *North Carolina Ghosts: They Are among Us*. Springville, UT: Sweetwater, 2006.

Harden, John. *The Devil's Tramping Ground and Other North Carolina Mystery Stories*. Chapel Hill: University of North Carolina Press, 1949.

Harden, John. *Tar Heel Ghosts*. Chapel Hill: University of North Carolina Press, 1954.

Lee, Robert E. *Blackbeard the Pirate: A Reappraisal of His Life and Times*. Winston-Salem, NC: John F. Blair, 1974.

Norton, Terry L. *Cherokee Myths and Legends*. Jefferson, NC: McFarland, 2014.

Priek, Brooks Newton. *Haunted Wilmington and the Cape Fear Coast: A Collection of "True" Ghost Stories*. Wrightsville Beach, NC: Banks Channel Books, 1995.

Renegar, Michael, and Amy Spease. *Ghosts of the Triad: Tales from the Heart of the Piedmont*. Haunted America. Charleston, SC: Arcadia, 2011.

Rivers, Michaels. *Appalachia Mountain Folklore*. Atglen, PA: Schiffer, 2012.

Roberts, Nancy. *North Carolina Ghosts & Legends*. Columbia: University of South Carolina Press, 1992.

Russell, Randy, and Janet Barnett. *Mountain Ghost Stories and Curious Tales of Western North Carolina*. Winston-Salem, NC: John F. Blair, 1988.

Sayad, Deonna Kelli. *Paranormal Obsession: America's Fascination with Ghosts & Haunting, Spooks & Spirits*. Woodbury, MN: Llewellyn, 2011.

Schlosser, S. E. *Spooky North Carolina: Tales of Haunting, Strange Happenings, and Other Local Lore*. Guilford, CT: Globe Pequot, 2009.

Tanenbaum, Linda Hunt, and Barry McGee. *Ghost Tales from the North Carolina Piedmont*. Winston-Salem, NC: Bandit Books, 2002.

Whedbee, Charles Harry. *Legends of the Outer Banks and Tar Heel Tidewater*. Winston-Salem, NC: John F. Blair, 1966.

Whedbee, Charles Harry. *Pirates, Ghosts, and Coastal Lore: The Best of Judge Whedbee*. Winston-Salem, NC: John F. Blair, 2004.

Zepke, Terrance. *Best Ghost Tales of North Carolina*. Sarasota, FL: Pineville, 2006.

ABOUT THE AUTHORS

Photo by Zack Fox

Jeffrey Cochran (left) is the researcher and writer of *The Carolina Haints Podcast*. Jeffrey runs a film, music, and print media production company called A Darker World. He has served as a writer and producer on multiple short films, including *Trouble Will Cause*, *Countdown to Midnight*, and *Uncle Otto's Truck*. Jeffrey attended North Carolina State University and has worked in aerospace engineering for twenty-two years. Jeffrey's first novel, *Sympathy for the Devil*, is strategically hidden among the millions of other books on Amazon Kindle.

Dan Sellers is the host and producer of *The Carolina Haints Podcast*. Dan is also the president and founder of Wreak Havoc Productions, a small film production company in Greensboro, North Carolina. He has written, produced, and directed multiple feature-length and short films, including *Uncle Otto's Truck*, *Midnight Shift*, and *Hank vs. the Undead*. Dan also serves as the festival director for the annual Wreak Havoc Horror Film Festival, an international showcase of independent horror cinema. He attended college at the University of North Carolina at Charlotte and has graduate degrees from the University of North Carolina at Greensboro and the Chicago School of Professional Psychology. Dan began a career in public service with the City of High Point, North Carolina, in 2009. He lives in Greensboro with his wife, Lauren, and their three children.